IAN HAY

THE
LIGHTER SIDE
OF SCHOOL LIFE

John Catt Educational Ltd

First published by T N Foulis in 1914
This edition published in 2006

*Published by permission of Samuel French Ltd
on behalf of the Estate of Ian Hay.*

ISBN: 1 904724 42 6

John Catt Educational Ltd
Great Glemham, Saxmundham, Suffolk IP17 2DH, UK
Tel: 01728 663666 Fax: 01728 663415
E-mail: enquiries@johncatt.co.uk Website: www.johncatt.com
Managing Director: Jonathan Evans – Editor in Chief: Derek Bingham

Printed and bound in Great Britain
by Bell & Bain, Glasgow, Scotland

CONTENTS

CHAP.		PAGE
	INTRODUCTION Nigel Richardson	5
	Jonty Driver	8
1	THE HEADMASTER	11
2	THE HOUSEMASTER	27
3	SOME FORM-MASTERS	38
4	BOYS	55
5	THE PURSUIT OF KNOWLEDGE	70
6	SCHOOL STORIES	84
7	"MY PEOPLE"	97
8	THE FATHER OF THE MAN	114

To
The Members
of
The Most Responsible
The Least Advertised
The Worst Paid
and
The Most Richly Rewarded
Profession
in the World

Acknowledgements

Following the successful re-publication of G. F. Bradby's *The Lanchester Tradition* in 2003, there were various suggestions as to which title we might consider next. That it is Ian Hay's *The Lighter Side of School Life*, first published in 1914, is due to two people.

Sincere thanks go to Nigel Richardson, Head of The Perse School, Cambridge, for proposing the book and supplying copy; and to Jonty Driver, former Master of Wellington College, for his research into the life of the author and for successfully tracking down the executors of his estate. Their Introductions, which appear on the following pages, add welcome perspective both to the era when it was written and to the author.

Our thanks also go to Amanda Smith, Editorial Director of Samuel French Ltd on behalf of the Estate of Ian Hay, for their permission to reprint it and for her encouragement.

INTRODUCTION

THE LIGHTER SIDE OF SCHOOL LIFE

IN AN essay which first appeared in *The Times* in 1975, Harold Macmillan (Prime Minister of Great Britain 1957-63) reflected on his own education at the turn of the twentieth century. He had been sent to prep school at Summer Fields, Oxford in the Lent Term of 1903; five years later he would move on to Eton, before returning to Oxford in 1911, and then being wounded in the Battle of the Somme. Macmillan's opening words were:

'Talleyrand once said that no one who had not lived in France before the Revolution could understand or have enjoyed *La douceur de vivre*. This dictum applies with equal force to anyone who cannot remember England before the First World War.'

It is against this background that Ian Hay's *The Lighter Side of School Life*, written in 1914 as the Great Powers prepared to go to war, must be seen – a wry, sideways glance at a carefree age in schools: one with a golden glow, soon to be extinguished.

In the decades before 1890, many of the great schools (those led by such eminent headmasters as Arnold and Thring) had established themselves as national institutions. Some had reinvented themselves from being erstwhile small country grammar schools into boarding schools serving the sons of the new, confidently optimistic and economically successful middle classes.

In the two decades which followed, a hearty, philathletic preoccupation with games and the newly emergent Combined Cadet Force (CCF) had been very marked. Their headmasters were similarly confident – and were portrayed in fictional form by writers such as E. W. Hornung in *Fathers of Men* (1912).

Vera Brittain's *Testament of Youth* (1933) gives us one contemporary picture – and describes her discovery of true but cruelly short-lived love. She wrote of the last pre-war speech day at Uppingham that year: that it was 'the one perfect summer idyll that I ever experienced'. By contrast, within only a few months the schools had begun to compile long lists of Old Boy casualties which would line the memorials on chapel walls once the war was over, and which would break the heart of many a headmaster or assistant master who studied them.

George Howson at Greshams was one such: Sue Smart's book *When Heroes Die* (2001) describes how Howson's health and spirit were broken by such losses. The fictional David Powlett-Jones, who began his teaching career less than a decade later in R. F. Delderfield's *To Serve Them all my Days* (1972) is a man bitterly hardened by his experiences of the Great War. He arrives at his new school to be shown a photograph by one of his new colleagues:

> 'That was our 1913 First Fifteen. Twelve are dead, and one of those survivors is legless. We've lost eighty-seven to date, seventy-two of them known to me personally. My boys...'

The post-war years would not be easy for these schools, as they battled first with the psychological effects of the Great War and then with a changing world dominated by economic depression. In reality, it was all a far cry from the scrapes and japes of Billy Bunter chronicled by Frank Richards through 60 years and 72 million words until his death in 1961.

And yet, as one re-reads Ian Hay, many of the figures whom he describes are not a million miles removed from Greyfriars' gentle and kindly headmaster, Dr Locke, or even from Bunter's form master, the terrifying Henry Samuel Quelch. A second world war, and the '60s social revolution which followed it, swept away many of the trappings which Hay describes, as schools had to adapt to rapidly changing times and transformed attitudes to authority.

Thus *The Lighter Side of School Life* transports us back into an age (real or imaginary) which has long since passed. There are few headmasters with private means; fewer who, having 'run a great public school, can run an empire' – although it is significant that even as early as 1914 Hay could write that a headmaster had to be 'essentially a man of business'. Many of us will have worked with some of the types of housemaster described in chapter two; some of us will have been taught by look-a-likes of form-master Mr. Wellings in chapter three.

Meanwhile management of change, and of people in times of change (not quite the same thing), are themes on most training courses for new heads. Those striving to achieve these things feature in many novels, plays and whodunits based in educational institutions – for example, Terence Rattigan's Dr. Frobisher (*The Browning Version*, 1948) or G. F. Bradby's Rev. Septimus Flaggon (*The Lanchester Tradition*, also 1914). C. P. Snow explored similar themes in *The Masters*; so did Alan Bennett in *The History Boys*; Tom Sharpe in *Porterhouse Blue* pitted the reforming Sir Godber and Lady Mary Evans against the conservative and resourceful Skullion. Many of the central characters in such books, both real and fictional, could have done with some of the shrewdness and insight which Hay reveals in observing those who work in such communities.

Above all, Hay describes the huge variety of expertise needed in any era by those who run schools or teach in them: political and psychological, sympathetic and diplomatic, as well as practical. He presents us with an enduring reminder of the variety of expertise that those who do our job still have to aspire to – political and psychological, sympathetic and diplomatic, as well as practical – abilities that remain remarkably unchanged from one generation to the next. In an age which prizes specialisation so much, the good schoolmaster remains a generalist.

Moreover, they are abilities which remain remarkably unchanged from one generation to the next. The *douceur* may have long since gone, but the essence of the job which we do remains much as it was in the Hay's time. He still has much to teach us.

Nigel Richardson

INTRODUCTION

IAN HAY

IAN HAY was the pseudonym of John Hay Beith (1876-1952), schoolmaster, soldier, novelist, playwright. It is odd that there has never been a full-scale biography written about him, because he was an interesting and complicated character, and successful in all four of those professional categories.

Educated at Fettes in Edinburgh and then at St John's College, Cambridge, first in classics, then in the sciences, he taught at Durham School for four years (1902-6) and at Fettes for six (1906-12). He coached rugby and rowing, and was a keen and (judging by his novels) knowledgeable cricketer.

In the First World War, he was a gallant front-line soldier, mentioned in dispatches in 1915 and winning the MC in 1916. By the end of that war he had been awarded a CBE and had reached the rank of major. In 1938, he published *The King's Service*, an informal history of the British army, and from 1938-41 he was director of public relations for the War Office, with the rank of major-general.

His first novel, *Pip, A Romance of Youth* (1907) was a best seller, as was *The First Hundred Thousand* (1916), an informal account (history is too strong a word) of Kitchener's army of the trenches – and he wrote more novels and informal histories, both before the First World War and after, and went on writing until his death in 1952.

In 1915, Hay married Helen Margaret Speirs; they had no children.

After 1919, he became a successful playwright. Not only did he adapt his own novels for the stage (his most successful play, *Tilly of Bloomsbury*, was based on his novel *Happy-Go-Lucky*, and *The Housemaster* – still performed by school dramatic societies – on the novel of the same title), he collaborated successfully with writers like Stephen King-Hall and P. G. Wodehouse in adapting their novels for the stage. *David and Destiny*, Ian Hay's novel of 1934, has a gracious dedication 'to my friend P. G. Wodehouse under whose remorseless goadings I have at last contrived to finish this book after seven years of labour grievously interrupted by periodical digressions (thrice in his company) into other and more frivolous fields of endeavour'.

At least two of Hay's plays were made into films and, in 1935, his success as a writer was confirmed by the boast of his publishers, by then Hodder and Stoughton, that: 'Over two million six hundred thousand copies of Ian Hay's books have now been sold'. He was chairman of the Society of Authors (1921-4 and again 1935-9), president of the Dramatists Club, and a celebrated figure in London society; a splendid portrait hangs in the Garrick Club.

The *New DNB* says of him: 'He was noted for charm, striking personality, equable temperament, after-dinner speeches, and personal austerity', though it notes too some evidence of personal unhappiness, and that the books of the last years of his life were not nearly as successful as those written in the first three-quarters. His one serious play, *Hattie Stowe* (1947), about the American reformer, Harriet Beecher Stowe, was a failure.

The Lighter Side of School Life, first published in 1914, was one of his early successes. It is neither novel, nor history, nor play, but a good-humoured report on and study of some of what Ian Hay had discovered about schools during his time as a schoolmaster. The 'heavier' side of school life would be the academic – the actual subject-teaching, what would now be called the 'curriculum'.

What might most surprise a modern reader of *The Lighter Side of School Life* is the omission of any mention of parents. Most of the other people whom one might expect to find in a school appear, directly or indirectly; but, in this boarding school world, parents are for babyhood, and then for the holidays. In term-time, their only existence is as the recipients of (often unwillingly written) weekly letters, the stamps for which are obtained from headmaster (in the prep school) or housemaster (in the public school).

Corporal punishment – including that administered by senior pupils to juniors – is accepted as a matter of course, though the justice or otherwise of the punishment isn't. It is a matter of course, too, that boys settle their arguments with their fists. A master's classroom is a private preserve, which even the headmaster enters only after knocking and waiting for an invitation. The idea that anyone should 'observe' another teacher's lesson, whether as inspector or mentor, would seem absurd. Moreover, the 'school life' is that of boys, not girls – moreover, boys in public (*ie* boarding) schools.

Perhaps these assumptions will make it seem that *The Lighter Side of School Life* is merely of historical interest, and that the book is thoroughly 'dated'. The extraordinary thing, however, is that in so many ways the apparently prelapsarian 'school life' which Ian Hay describes still exists now. Schoolboys have the same lessons to learn (lessons which have little to do with the subjects they are taught). Monitors and prefects have to learn to lead. Bullies have to be faced – and defeated. Teachers have to learn how to control their classes. Headmasters have to learn that justice which is not dispensed even-handedly often seems worse than injustice. Throughout the book, Ian Hay tells stories, for the most memorable moral teaching nearly always involves the telling of good stories.

Re-reading *The Lighter Side of School Life* is not, in other words, merely an exercise in nostalgia (though some readers may look back at the orderly world of 1900-1914 with longing): this isn't just the world we have lost; it is the good-humoured and worldly wisdom of someone who understood schools – especially boarding schools – from the inside out. Of course we have to read critically and historically; but anyone with any experience of schools (not only in the United Kingdom, but in any of the countries influenced by British education) will find himself, nearly 100 years later, saying, again and again, "It's still exactly the same".

That shouldn't be a surprise, really: we suppose that institutions change faster than they actually do – and as we grow older we learn that human nature, even if it does change, does so very slowly indeed.

Jonty Driver

Chapter One

THE HEADMASTER

First of all there is the Headmaster of Fiction. He is invariably called "The Doctor", and he wears cap and gown even when birching malefactors – which he does intermittently throughout the day – or attending a cricket match. For all we know he wears them in bed.

He speaks a language peculiar to himself – a language which at once enables you to recognise him as a Headmaster; just as you may recognise a stage Irishman from the fact that he says "Begorrah!", or a stage sailor from the fact that he has to take constant precautions with his trousers. Thus, the "Doctor" invariably addresses his cowering pupils as "Boys!" – a form of address which in reality only survives nowadays in places where you are invited to "have another with me" – and if no audience of boys is available at the moment, he addresses a single boy as if he were a whole audience. To influential parents he is servile and oleaginous, and he treats his staff with fatuous pomposity. Such a being may have existed – may exist – but we have never met him.

What of the Headmaster of Fact? To condense him into a type is one of the most difficult things in the world, for this reason. Most of us have known only one Headmaster in our lives – if we have known more we are not likely to say so, for obvious reasons – and it is difficult for Man (as distinct from Woman), to argue from the particular to the general. Moreover, the occasions upon which we have met the subject of our researches at close quarters have not been favourable to dispassionate character-study. It is difficult to form an unbiased or impartial judgment of a man out of material supplied solely by a series of brief interviews spread over a period of years – interviews at which his contribution to the conversation has been limited to a curt request that you will bend over, and yours to a sequence of short sharp ejaculations.

However, some of us have known more than one Headmaster, and upon us devolves the solemn duty of distilling our various experiences into a single essence.

What are the characteristics of a *great* Headmaster? Instinct at once prompts us to premise that he must be a scholar and a gentleman. A gentleman, undoubtedly, he must be; but nowadays scholarship – high classical scholarship – is a hindrance rather than a help. To supervise the instruction of modern youth a man requires something more than profound learning: he must possess *savoir faire*. If you set a great scholar – and a great scholar has an unfortunate habit of being nothing but a great scholar – in charge of the multifarious interests of a public school, you are setting a razor to cut grindstones. As well appoint an Astronomer Royal to command an Atlantic liner. He may be on terms of easy familiarity with the movements of the heavenly bodies, yet fail to understand the right way of dealing with refractory stokers.

A Headmaster is too busy as personage to keep his own scholarship tuned up to concert pitch; and if he devotes adequate time to this object – and a scholar must practise almost as diligently as a pianist or an acrobat if he is to remain in the first flight – he will have little leisure left for less intellectual but equally vital duties. Nowadays in great public schools the Head, although he probably takes the Sixth for an hour or two a day, delegates most of his work in this direction to a capable and up-to-date young man fresh from the University, and devote his energies to such trifling details as the organisation of school routine, the supervision of the cook, the administration of justice, the diplomatic handling of the Governing Body, and the suppression of parents.

So far then we are agreed – the great advantage of dogmatising in print is that one can take the agreement of the reader for granted – that a Headmaster must be a gentleman, but not necessarily a scholar – in the very highest sense of the word. What other virtues must he possess? Well, he must be a majestic figurehead. This is not so difficult as it sounds. The dignity which doth hedge a Headmaster is so tremendous that the dullest and fussiest of the race can hardly fail to be impressive and awe-inspiring to the plastic mind of youth. More than one King Log has left a name behind him, through standing still in the limelight and keeping his mouth shut. But then he was probably lucky in his lieutenants.

Next, he must have a sense of humour. If he cannot see the entertaining side of youthful depravity, magisterial jealousy, and parental fussiness, he will undoubtedly go mad. A sense of humour, too, will prevent him from making a fool of himself, and a Headmaster must never do that. It also endangers Tact, and Tact is the essence of life to a man who has to deal every day with the ignorant, and the bigoted, and the sentimental. (These adjectives are applicable to boys, masters, and parents, and may be applied collectively or individually with equal truth.) Not that all humorous people are tactful: bitter experience of the practical joker has taught us that. But no person can be tactful who cannot see the ludicrous side of things. There is a certain Headmaster of today, justly celebrated as a brilliant teacher and a born organiser, who is lacking – entirely lacking – in that priceless gift of the gods, a sense of humour, with which is incorporated Tact. Shortly after he took up his present appointment, one of the most popular boys in the school, while leading the field in a cross-country race, was run over and killed by an express train which emerged from a tunnel as he ran across the line, within measurable distance of accomplishing a record for the course.

Next morning the order went forth that the whole school were to assemble in the great hall. They repaired thither, not unpleasantly thrilled. There would be a funeral oration, and boys are curiously partial to certain forms of emotionalism. They liked to be harangued before a football-match, for instance, in the manner of the Greeks of old. These boys had already had a taste of the Head's quality as a speaker, and they felt that he would do their departed hero justice. They reminded one another of the moving words which the late Head had spoken when an Old Boy had fallen in battle a few years before under particularly splendid circumstances. They remembered how pleased the Old Boy's father and mother had been about it. Their comrade, whom they had revered and loved as recently as yesterday, would receive a fitting farewell too; and they would all feel the prouder of the school for the words that they were about hear. They did not say this aloud, for the sentimentality of boys is of the inarticulate kind, but the thought was uppermost in their minds.

Presently they were all assembled, and the Head appeared upon his rostrum. There was a deathlike stillness: not a boy stirred.

Then the Head spoke.

"Any boy," he announced, "found trespassing upon the railway line in future will be expelled. You may go."

They went. The organisation of that school is still a model of perfection, and its scholarship list is exceptionally high. But the school has never forgiven the Head, and never will so long as tradition and sentiment count for anything in this world.

So far, then, we have accumulated the following virtues for the Headmaster. He must be a gentleman, a picturesque figure-head, and must possess a good sense of humour.

He must also, of course, be a ruler. Now you may rule men in two ways – either with a rapier or a bludgeon; but a man who can gain his ends with the latter will seldom have recourse to the former. The Headmaster who possesses on the top of other essential qualities the power of being uncompromisingly and divinely rude, is to be envied above all men. For him life is full of short cuts. He never argues. "*L'ecole, c'est moi,*" he growls, and no one contradicts him. Boys idolise him. In his presence they are paralysed with fear, but away from it they glory in his ferocity of mien and strength of arm. Masters rave impotently at his *brusquerie* and absolutism. "Well, it's a treat to see the way the old man keeps B and C up to the collar." As for parents, they simply refuse to face him, which is the head and summit of that which a master desires of a parent.

Such a man is Olympian, having none of the foibles or soft moments of a human being. He dwells apart, in an atmosphere too rarefied for those who intrude into it. His subjects never regard him as a man of like passions with themselves: they would be quite shocked if such an idea were suggested to them. I once asked a distinguished *alumnus* of a great school, which had been ruled with consummate success for twenty four years by such a Head as I have described, to give me a few reminiscences of the great man as a *man* – his characteristics, his mannerisms, his vulnerable points, his tricks of expression, his likes and dislikes, and his hobbies.

My friend considered.

"He *was* a holy terror," he announced, after profound meditation.

"Quite so. But in what way?"

My friend thought again.

"I can't remember anything particular about him," he said, "except that he was a holy terror – and the greatest man that ever lived!"

"But tell me something personal about him. How did his conversation impress you?"

"*Conversation?* Bless you, he never *conversed* with anybody. He just told them what he thought about a thing and that settled it. Besides, I never exchanged a word with him in my life. But he was a great man."

"Didn't you meet him all the time you were at school?"

"Oh yes, I *met* him," replied my friend with feeling – "three or four times. And that reminds me, I *can* tell you something personal about him. The old swine was left-handed! A great man, a great man!"

Happy the warrior who can inspire worship on such sinister foundations as these!

The other kind has to prevail by another method – the Machiavellian. As a successful Headmaster of my acquaintance once brutally but truthfully expressed it: "You simply have to employ a certain amount of low cunning if you are going to keep a school going at all." And he was right. A man unendowed with his divine gift of rudeness would, if he spent his time answering the criticisms or meeting the objections of colleagues or parents or even boys, have no time for anything else. So he seeks refuge either in finesse or flight. If a parent rings him up on the telephone, he murmurs something courteous about a wrong number and then leaves the receiver off the hook. If a housemaster, swelling with some grievance or scheme of reform, bears down upon him upon the cricket field on a summer afternoon, he adroitly lures him under a tree where another housemaster is standing, and leaves them there together. If an enthusiastic junior discharges at his head some glorious but quite impracticable project, such as the performance of a pastoral play in the school grounds, or the enforcement of a vegetarian diet upon the School for experimental purposes, he replies: "My dear fellow, the Governing Body will never hear of it!" What he means is: "The Governing Body shall never hear of it."

He has other diplomatic resources at his call. Here is an example.

A Headmaster once called his flock together and said:

"A very unpleasant and discreditable thing has happened. The municipal authorities have recently erected a pair of extremely ornate and expensive – er – lamp-posts outside the residence of the Mayor of the town. These lamp-posts appear to have attracted the unfavourable notice of the School. Last Sunday evening, between seven and eight o'clock, they were attacked and wrecked, apparently by volleys of stones."

There was a faint but appreciative murmur from those members of the School to whom the news of this outrage was now made public for the first time. But a baleful flash from the Head's spectacles restored instant silence.

"Several parties of boys," he continued, "must have passed these lamp-posts on that evening, on their way back to their respective houses after Chapel. I wish to see all boys who in any way participated in the outrage in my study directly after Second School. I warn them that I shall make a severe example of them." His voice rose to a blare. "I will not have the prestige and fair fame of the School lowered in the eyes of the Town by the vulgar barbarities of a parcel of ill-conditioned little street-boys. You may go!"

The audience rose to their feet and began to steal silently away. But they were puzzled. The Old Man was no fool as a rule. Did he really imagine that chaps would be such mugs as to own up?

But before the first boy reached the door the Head spoke again.

"I may mention," he added very gently, "that the attack upon the – er – lamp-posts was witnessed by a gentleman resident in the neighbourhood, a warm friend of the School. He was able to identify *one* of the culprits, whose name is in my possession. That is all."

And enough too! When the Head visited his study after Second School, he found seventeen malefactors meekly awaiting chastisement.

But he never divulged the name of the boy who had been identified, or for that matter, the identity of the warm friend of the School. I *wonder*!

One more quality is essential to the great Headmaster. He must possess the Sixth Sense. He must see nothing, yet know everything that goes on in the School. Etiquette forbids that he should enter one of his colleague's houses except as an invited guest; yet he must be acquainted with all that happens inside that house. He is debarred by the same rigid law from entering the form-room or studying the methods and capability of any but the most junior form-masters; and yet he must know whether Mr. A. in the Senior Science Set is expounding theories of inorganic chemistry which have been obsolete for ten years, or whether Mr. B. in the Junior Remove is accustomed meekly to remove a pool of ink from the seat of his chair before beginning his daily labours. He must not mingle with the boys, for that would be undignified; yet he must, and usually does, know every boy in the School by sight, and something about him. He must never attempt to acquire information by obvious cross-examination either of boy or master, or he will be accused of prying and interference; and he can never, or should never, discuss one of his colleagues with another. And yet he must have his hand upon the pulse of the School in such wise as to be able to tell which master is incompetent, which prefect is untrustworthy, which boy is a bully, and which House is rotten. In other words, he must possess a Red Indian's powers of observation and a woman's powers of intuition. He must be able to suck in school atmosphere through his pores. He must be able to judge of a man's keenness or his fitness for duty by his general attitude and conversation when off duty. He must be able to read volumes from the demeanour of a group in the corner of the quadrangle, from a small boy's furtive expression or even from the *timbre* of the singing in chapel. He must notice which boy has too many friends and which none at all.

Such are a few of the essentials of the great Headmaster, and to the glory of our system be it said that there are still many in the land. But the type is changing. The autocratic Titan of the past has been shorn of his locks by two Delilahs – Modern Sides and Government Interference.

First, Modern Sides.

Time was when A Sound Classical Education, Lady Matron, and Meat for Breakfast formed the alpha and omega of a public school prospectus. But times have changed, at least in so far as the Sound Classical Education is concerned. The Headmaster of the old school, who looks upon the classics as the foundation of all education, and regards modern sides as a sop to the parental Cerberus, finds himself called upon to cope with new and strange monsters.

First of all, the members of that once despised race, the teachers of Science. Formerly these maintained a servile and apologetic existence, supervising a turbulent collection of young gentlemen whose sole appreciation of this branch of knowledge was derived from the unrivalled opportunities which its pursuit afforded for the creation of horrible stenches and untimely explosions. Now they have uprisen, and, asseverating that classical education is a pricked bubble, ask boldly for expensive apparatus and a larger tract of space in the time-table.

Then the parent. He has got quite out of hand lately. In days past things were different. Usually an old public-school boy himself, and proudly conscious that Classics had made him "what he was", the parent deferred entirely to the Headmaster's judgment, and entrusted his son to his care without question or stipulation. But a new race of parents has arisen, men who avow, modestly but firmly, that they have been made not by the Classics but by themselves, and who demand, with a great assumption of you-can't-put-*me*-off-with-last-season's-goods, that their offspring shall be taught something up-to-date – something which will be "useful" in an office.

Again, there is our old friend the Man in the Street who, through the medium of his favourite mouthpiece, the halfpenny press, asks the Headmaster very sternly what he means by turning out "scholars" who are incapable of writing an invoice in commercial Spanish, and to whom double entry is Double Dutch.

And lastly, there is the boy himself, whose utter loathing and horror of education as a whole has not blinded him to the fact that the cultivation of some branches thereof calls for considerably less effort than that of others, and who accordingly occupies the greater part of his weekly letter home with fervent requests to his parents to permit him to drop Classics and take up modern languages or science.

The united agitations of this incongruous band have called into existence the Modern Side – Delilah Number One. Now for Number Two. Until a few years ago the State confined its ebullience in matters educational to the Board Schools. But with the growth of national education and class jealousy – the two seem to go hand-in-hand – the working classes of this country began to point out to the Government, not altogether unreasonably, that what is sauce for the goose is sauce for the gander. "Why," they inquired bitterly, "should *we* be the only people educated? Must the poor *always* be oppressed, while the rich go free? What about these public schools of yours – the seminaries of the bloated and pampered Aristocracy? You leave us alone for a bit, and give them a turn, or we may get nasty!" So a pliable Government, remembering that public school masters are not represented in Parliament while the working-classes are, obeyed. They began by publicly announcing that in future all teachers must be trained to teach. To give effect to this decree, they declared their intention of immediately introducing a Bill to provide that after a certain date no Headmaster of any school, high or low, would be permitted to engage an assistant who had not earned a certificate at a training college and registered himself in a mysterious schedule called 'Column B', paying a guinea for the privilege.

The prospective schoolmasters of the day – fourth-year men at Oxford and Cambridge, inexperienced in the ways of Government Departments – were deeply impressed. Most of them hurriedly borrowed a guinea and registered in Column B. They even went further. In the hope of forestalling the foolish virgins of their profession, they attended lectures and studied books which deal with the science of education. They came *attachés* at East End Board-Schools, where, under the supervision of a capable but plebeian Master of Method, they endeavoured to instruct classes of some sixty or seventy babbling six-year-olds in the elements of reading and writing in order that hereafter they might be better able to elucidate Cicero and Thucydides to scholarship candidates at a public school.

Others, however – the aforementioned foolish virgins – whose knowledge of British politics was greater than their interest in the Theory of Education, decided to 'wait and see'. That is to say, they accepted the first vacancy at a public school which presented itself and settled down to work upon the old lines, a year's seniority to the good. In a just world this rashness and improvidence would have met with its due reward – namely, ultimate eviction (when the Bill passed) from a comfortable berth, and a stern command to go and learn the business of teaching before presuming to teach. But unfortunately the Bill never did pass: it never so much as reached its First Reading. It lies now in some dusty pigeon-hole in the Education Office, forgotten by all save its credulous victims. The British Exchequer is the richer by several thousand guineas, contributed by a class to whom, of course, a guinea is a mere bagatelle; and here and there throughout the public schools of this country there exist men who, when they first joined the Staff, had the mysterious formula, "Reg. Col. B." printed upon their testimonials, and discoursed learnedly to stupefied Headmasters about brain-tracks and psychology, and the mutual stimulus of co-sexual competition, for a month or two before awakening to the one fundamental truth which governs public-school education – namely, that if you can keep boys in order you can teach them anything; if not, all the Column B.'s in the Education Office will avail you nothing.

That was all. The incident is ancient history now. It was a capital practical joke, perpetuated by a Government singularly lacking in humour in other respects; and no one remembers it except the people to whom the guineas belong. But it gave the Headmasters of the country a bad fright. It provides them with a foretaste of the nuisance which the State can make of itself when it chooses to be paternal. So such of the Headmasters as were wise decided to be upon their guard for the future against the blandishments of the party politician. And they were justified; for presently the Legislature stirred in its sleep and embarked upon yet another enterprise.

Philip, king of Macedon, used to say that no city was impregnable whose gates were wide enough to admit a single mule-load of gold.

Similarly the Board of Education decided that no public school, however haughty or exclusive, could ever again call its soul its own once the Headmaster (of his own free will, or overruled by the Governing Body) had been asinine enough to accept a "grant". So they approached the public schools with fair words. They said:

"How would you like a subsidy, now, wherewith to build a new science laboratory? What about a few State-aided scholarships? Won't you let us help you? Strict secrecy will be observed, and advances made upon your note of hand alone" – or words to that effect.

The larger and better-endowed public schools, conscious of a fat bank-balance and a long waiting list of prospective pupils, merely winked their rheumy eyes and shook their heavy heads.

"*Timeo Danaos*," they growled – "*et dona ferentes*."

When this observation was translated to the Minister for Education, he smiled enigmatically, and bided his time. But some of the smaller schools, hard pressed by modern competition, gobbled the bait at once. The mule-load of gold arrived promptly, and close in its train came Retribution. Inspectors swooped down – clerkly young men who in their time had passed an incredible number of Standards, and were now receiving what was to them a princely salary for indulging in the easiest and most congenial of all human recreations – that of criticising the efforts of others. There arrived, too, precocious prize-pupils from the Board Schools, winners of County Council scholarships which entitled them to a few years' "polish" at a public school – a polish but slowly attained, despite constant friction with their new and loving playmates.

But the great strongholds still held out. So other methods were adopted. The examination screw was applied.

As most of us remember to our cost, we used periodically in our youth at school to suffer from an "examination week", during which a mysterious power from outside was permitted to inflict upon us examination papers upon every subject upon earth, under the title of Oxford and Cambridge Locals – the High, the Middle, and the Low – or, in Scotland, the Leaving Certificate. These papers were set and corrected by persons unknown, residing in London; and we were supervised as we answered them not by our own preceptors – they stampeded joyously away to play golf – but by strange creatures who took charge of the examination room with an air of uneasy assurance, suggestive of a man travelling first-class with a third-class ticket. In due course the results were declared; and the small school which gained a large percentage of Honourable Mentions was able to underline the fact heavily in its prospectus. These examinations were, if not organised, at least recognised by the State; and once they had pierced the battlements of a school an Inspector invariably crawled through the breach after them. Henceforth that school was subject to periodical visitations and reports.

Naturally the Headmasters of the great public schools clanged their gates and dropped their portcullises against such an infraction of the law that a Headmaster's school is his castle. But, as already mentioned, the screw was applied. The certificates awarded to successful candidates in these examinations were made the key to higher things. Three Higher Grade Certificates, for instance, were accepted in *lieu* of certain subjects in Oxford Smalls and Cambridge Little-go. The State pounced upon this principle and extended it. The acquisition of a sufficient number of these certificates now paved the way to various State services. Extra marks or special favours were awarded to young gentlemen who presented themselves for Sandhurst or Woolwich or the Civil Service bringing their sheaves with them in the form of Certificates. Roughly speaking, the more Certificates a candidate produced the more enthusiastically he was excused from the necessity of learning the elements of his trade.

The governing bodies of various professions took up the idea. For instance, if you produced four Higher Certificates – say for Geography, Botany, Electro-Dynamics and Practical Cookery – you were excused the preliminary examination of the Society of Chartered Accountants. (We need not pin ourselves down to the absolute accuracy of these details: they are merely for purposes of illustration.) Anyhow, it was a beautiful idea. A Headmaster of my acquaintance once assured me that he believed that the possession of a complete set of Higher Grade Certificates for all the Local Examinations of a single year would entitle the holder to a seat in the reformed House of Lords.

In other words, it was still possible to get into the Universities and Services without Certificates, but it was very much easier to get in with them.

So the great Headmasters climbed down. But they made terms. They would accept the Local Examinations, and they would admit Inspectors within their fastnesses; but they respectfully but firmly insisted upon having some sort of say in the choice of the Inspector.

The Government met them more than halfway. In fact, they fell in with the plan with suspicious heartiness.

"Certainly, my dear sir," they said: "you shall choose your own Inspector; and what is more, you shall *pay* him! Think of that! The man will be a mere tool in your hands – a hired servant – and you can do what you like with him."

It was an ingenious and comforting way of putting things, and may be commended to the notice of persons writhing in a dentist's chair; for it forms an exact parallel: the description applies to dentist and inspector equally. However, the Headmasters agreed to it; and now all our great schools receive inspectorial visitations of some kind. That is to say, upon an appointed date a gentleman comes down from London, spends the day as the guest of the Headmaster; and after being conducted about the premises from dawn to dusk, departs in the gloaming with his brain in a fog and some sixteen guineas in his pocket.

He is a variegated type, this Super-Inspector. Frequently he is a clever man who has failed as a schoolmaster and now earns a comfortable living because he remembered in time the truth of the saying: *La critique est aisé, l'art difficile*. More often he is a superannuated University professor, with a penchant for irrelevant anecdote and a disastrous sense of humour. Sometimes he is aggressive and dictatorial, but more often (humbly remembering where he is and who is going to pay for all this) apprehensive, deferential and quite inarticulate. Sometime he is a scholar and a gentleman, with a real appreciation of the atmosphere of a public school and a sound knowledge of the principles of education. But not always. And whoever he is and whatever he is, the Head loathes him impartially and dispassionately.

Such are the thorns with which the pillow of a modern Headmaster is stuffed. His greatest stumbling-block is Tradition – the hoary edifices of convention and precedent, built up and jealously guarded by Old Boys and senior Housemasters. Of Parents we will treat in another place.

What is he like, the Headmaster of today?

Firstly and essentially, he is no longer a despot. He is a constitutional sovereign, like all other modern monarchs; and perhaps it is better so. Though a Head still exercises enormous personal power, for good or ill, a school no longer stands or falls by its Headmaster, as in the old days, any more than a country stands or falls by its King, as in the days of the Stuarts. Public opinion, Housemasters, the prefectorial system – these have combined to modify his absolutism. But though a bad Headmaster may not be able to wreck a good school, it is certain that no school can ever become great, or remain great, without a great man at the head of it.

Time has wrought other changes. Twenty years ago no man could ever hope to reach the summit of the scholastic universe who was not in Orders and the possessor of a First Class Classical degree. Now the layman, the modern-side man, above all the man of affairs, are raising their heads.

Under these new conditions, what manner of man is the great Head of today?

He is essentially a man of business. A clear brain and a sense of proportion enable him to devise schemes of education in which the old idealism and the new materialism are judiciously blended. He knows how to draw up a school time-table – almost as difficult and complicated a document as Bradshaw – making provision, hour by hour, day by day, for the teaching of a very large number of subjects by a limited number of men to some hundreds of boys all at different stages of progress, in such a way that no boy shall be left idle for a single hour and no master be called upon to be in two places at once.

He understands school finance and educational politics, which are even more peculiar than British party politics. He combines the art of being able to rule upon his own initiative for months at a time, and yet renders a satisfactory account of his stewardship to an ignorant and inquisitive Governing Body which meets twice a year.

He is, as ever, an imposing figure-head; and if he is, or has been, an athlete, so much the easier for him in his dealings with the boys. He possesses the art of managing men to an extent sufficient to maintain his Housemasters in some sort of line, and to keep his junior staff punctual and enthusiastic without fussing or herding them. He is a good speaker, and though not invariably in Orders, he appreciates the enormous influence that a powerful sermon in Chapel may exercise at a time of crisis; and he supplies that sermon himself.

He keeps a watchful eye upon an army of servants, and does not shrink from the drudgery of going through kitchen-accounts or laundry estimates. He investigates complaints personally, whether they have to do with a House's morals or a butler's perquisites.

He keeps abreast of the educational needs of the time. He is a *persona grata* at the Universities, and usually knows at which University and at which College thereof one of his boys will be most likely to win a scholarship. In the interests of the Army Class he maintains friendly relations with the War Office, because, in these days of the chronic reforms of that institution, to be in touch with the "permanent" military mind is to save endless trouble over examinations which are going to be dropped or schedules which are about to be abandoned before they come into operation. He cultivates the acquaintance of those in high places, not for his own advancement, but because it is good for the School to be able to bring down an occasional celebrity, to present prizes or open a new wing. For the same reason he dines out a good deal – often when he has been on his feet since seven o'clock in the morning – and entertains in return, so far as he can afford it, people who are likely to be able to do the School a good turn. For with him it is the School, the School, the School, all the time.

If he possesses private means of his own, so much the better; for the man with a little spare money in his pocket possesses powers of leverage denied to the man who has none. I know of a Headmaster who once shamed his Governing Body into raising the salaries of the Junior Staff to a decent standard by supplementing those salaries out of his own slender resources for something like five years.

And above all, he has sympathy and insight. When a master or boy comes to him with a grievance he knows whether he is dealing with a chronic grumbler or a wronged man. The grumbler can be pacified by a word or chastened by a rebuke; but a man burning under a sense of real injustice and wrong will never be efficient again until his injuries are redressed. If a colleague, again, comes to him with a scheme of work, or organisation, or even play, he is quick to see how far the scheme is valuable and practicable, and how far it is mere fuss and officiousness. He is enormously patient over this sort of thing, for he knows that an untimely snub may kill the enthusiasm of a real worker, and that a little encouragement may do wonders for a diffident beginner. He knows how to stimulate the slacker, be he boy or master; and he keeps a sharp look-out to see that the willing horse does not overwork himself. (This latter, strange as it may seem, is the harder task of the two.) And he can read the soul of that most illegible of books – save to the understanding eye – the boy, through and through. He can tell if a boy is lying brazenly, or lying because he is frightened, or lying to screen a friend, or speaking the truth. He knows when to be terrible in anger, and when to be indescribably gentle.

Usually he is slightly unpopular. But he does not allow this to trouble him overmuch, for he is a man who is content to wait for his reward. He remembers the historic verdict of "A beast, but a just beast" and chuckles.

Such a man is an Atlas, holding up a little world. He is always tired, for he can never rest. His so-called hours of ease are clogged by correspondence, most it quite superfluous, and the telephone has added a new terror to his life. But he is always cheerful, even when alone; and he loves his work. If he did not, it would kill him.

A Headmaster no longer regards his office as a stepping stone to a Bishopric. In the near future, as ecclesiastical and classical traditions fade, that office is more likely to be regarded as a qualification for a place at the head of a Department of State, or a seat in the Cabinet. A man who can run a great public school can run an Empire.

Chapter Two

THE HOUSEMASTER

To the boy, all masters (as distinct from The Head) consist of one class – namely, masters. The fact that masters are divisible into grades, or indulge in acrimonious diversities of opinion, or are subject to the ordinary weaknesses of the flesh (apart from chronic shortness of temper) has never occurred to him.

This is not so surprising as it sounds. A schoolmaster's life is one long pose. His perpetual demeanour is that of a blameless enthusiast. A boy never hears a master swear – at least, not if the master can help it; he seldom sees him smoke or drink; he never hears him converse upon any but regulation topics, and then only from the point of view of a rather bigoted archangel. The idea that a master in his private capacity may go to a music-hall, or back a horse, or be casual in his habits, or be totally lacking in religious belief, would be quite a shock to a boy.

It is true that when half a dozen ribald spirits are gathered round the Lower Study fire after tea, libellous tongues are unloosed. The humorist of the party draws joyous pictures of his Housemaster staggering home to bed after a riotous evening with an Archdeacon, or being thrown out of the Empire in the holidays. But no one in his heart takes these legends seriously – least of all their originator. They are merely audacious irreverences.

All day and every day the boy sees the master, impeccably respectable in cap and gown, rebuking the mildest vices, extolling the dullest virtues, singing the praises of industry and application, and attending Chapel morning and evening. A boy has little or no intuition: he judges almost entirely by externals. To him a master is not as other men are: he is a special type of humanity endowed with a permanent bias towards energetic respectability, and grotesquely ignorant of the seamy side of life. The latter belief in particular appears to be quite ineradicable.

But in truth the scholastic hierarchy is a most complicated fabric. At the summit of the Universe stands the Head. After him come the senior masters – or, as they prefer somewhat invidiously to describe themselves, the permanent staff – then the junior masters. The whole body are divided and subdivided again into little groups – classical men, mathematical men, science men, and modern-language men – each group with its own tender spots. Then follow various specialists, not always resident; men whose life is one long and usually ineffectual struggle to convince the School – including the Head – that music, drawing, and the arts generally are subjects which ought to be taken seriously, even under the British educational system.

As already noted, after the Head – quite literally – come the Housemasters. They are always after him: one or other of the troop is perpetually on his trail; and unless the great man displays the ferocity of the tiger or the wisdom of the serpent, they harry him exceedingly.

A., a patronising person, with a few helpful suggestions upon the general management of the School. He usually begins: "In the old Head's day, we never, under any circumstances–"

B., whose speciality is to discover motes in the eyes of other Housemasters. He announces that yesterday afternoon he detected a member of the Eleven fielding in a Panama hat. "Are Panama hats permitted by the statutes of the School? I need hardly say that the boy was not a member of my House."

C., a wobbler, who seeks advice as to whether an infraction of one of the rules of his House can best be met by a hundred lines of Vergil or public expulsion.

D., a Housemaster pure and simple, urging the postponement of the Final House-Match, D's best bowler having contracted an ingrowing toe-nail.

E., another, insisting that the date be adhered to – for precisely the same reason.

(He receives no visit from F., who holds that a Housemaster's House is his castle, and would as soon think of coming to the fountain-head for advice as he would of following the advice if it were offered.)

G., an alarmist, who has heard a rumour that smallpox has broken out in the adjacent village, and recommends that the entire school be vaccinated forthwith.

H., a golfer, suggesting a half-holiday, to celebrate some suddenly unearthed anniversary in the annals of Country or School.

Lastly, on the telephone, I., a valetudinarian, to announce that he is suffering from double pneumonia and will be unable to come into School until after luncheon.

To be quite just, I. is the rarest bird of all. The average schoolmaster has a perfect passion for sticking to his work when utterly unfit for it. In this respect he differs materially from his pupil, who lies in bed in the dawning hours, cudgelling his sleepy but fertile brain for a disease which

(1) Has not been used before.
(2) Will incapacitate him for work all morning.
(3) Will not prevent him playing football in the afternoon.

But if a master sprains his ankle, he hobbles about his form-room on a crutch. If he contracts influenza, he swallows a jorum of ammoniated quinine, puts on three waistcoats, and totters into school, where he proceeds to disseminate germs among his not ungrateful charges. Even if he is rendered speechless by tonsillitis, he takes his form as usual, merely substituting written invective (chalked up on the blackboard), for the torrent of verbal abuse which he usually employs as a medium of instruction.

It is all part – perhaps an unconscious part – of his permanent pose as an apostle of what is strenuous and praiseworthy. It is also due to a profound conviction that whoever of his colleagues is told off to take his form for him will indubitably undo the work of many years within a few hours.

Besides harrying the head and expostulating with one another, the Housemasters wage unceasing war with the teaching staff.

The bone of contention in every case is a boy, and the combat always follows certain well-defined lines.

A form-master overtakes a Housemaster hurrying to morning chapel, and inquires carelessly :

"By the way, isn't Binks tertius your boy?"

The Housemaster guardedly admits that this is so.

"Well, do you mind if I flog him?"

"Oh, come, I say, isn't that rather drastic? What has he done?"

"Nothing – not a hand'-turn – for six weeks."

"Um!" The Housemaster endeavours to look severely judicial. "Young Binks is rather an exceptional boy," he observes. (Young Binks always is.) "Are you quite sure you *know* him?"

The form-master, who has endured Master Binks' society for nearly two years and knows him only too well, laughs caustically.

"Yes," he says, "I do know him: and I quite agree with you that he is rather an exceptional boy."

"Ah!" says the Housemaster, falling into the snare. "Then –"

"An exceptional young swab," explains the form-master.

By this time they have entered the Chapel, where they revert to their daily task of setting an example by howling one another down in the Psalms.

After Chapel, the Housemaster takes the form-master aside and confides to him the intelligence that he has been a Housemaster for twenty-five years. The form-master, suppressing an obvious retort, endeavours to return to the question of Binks; but is compelled instead to listen to a brief homily upon the management of boys in general. As neither gentleman has breakfasted, the betting as to which will lose his temper first is almost even, with odds slightly in favour of the form-master, being the younger and hungrier man. However, it is quite certain that one of them will – probably both. The light of reason being thus temporarily obscured they part, to meditate further repartees and complain bitterly of one another to their colleagues.

But it is very seldom that Master Binks profits by such Olympian differences as these. Possibly the Housemaster may decline to give the form-master permission to flog Binks, but in nine cases out of ten, being nothing if not conscientious he flogs Binks himself, carefully explaining to the form-master afterwards, by implication only, that he has done so not from conviction, but from an earnest desire to bolster up the authority of an inexperienced and incompetent colleague. But these quibbles, as already observed, do not help the writhing Binks at all.

However, a Housemaster *contra mundum*, and a Housemaster in his own House, are very different beings. We have already seen that a bad Headmaster cannot always prevent a School from being good. But a House stands or falls entirely by its Housemaster. If he is a good Housemaster it is a good House: if not, nothing can save it. And therefore the responsibility of a Housemaster far exceeds that of a Head.

Consider. He is *in loco parentis* – with apologies to Stalky! – to some forty or fifty of the shyest and most reserved animals in the world; one and all animated by a single desire – namely, to prevent any fellow-creature from ascertaining what is at the back of their minds. Schoolgirls, we are given to understand, are prone to open their hearts to one another, or to some favourite teacher, with luxurious abandonment. Not so boys. Up to a point they are frankness itself: beyond that point lie depths which can only be plumbed by instinct and intuition – qualities whose possession is the only test of a born Housemaster. All his flock must be an open book to him: he must understand both its collective and its individual tendencies. If a boy is inert and listless, the Housemaster must know whether his condition is due to natural sloth or some secret trouble, such as bullying or evil companionship. If a boy appears dour and dogged, the Housemaster has to decide whether he is shy or merely insolent. Private tastes and pet hobbies must also be borne in mind. The complete confidence of a hitherto unresponsive subject can often be won by a tactful reference to music or photography. The Housemaster must be able, too, to distinguish between brains and mere precocity, and to separate the fundamentally stupid boy from the lazy boy who is pretending to be stupid – an extremely common type. He must cultivate a keen nose for the malingerer, and at the same time keep a sharp lookout for fear lest the conscientious plodder should plod himself silly. He must discriminate between the whole-hearted enthusiast and the pretentious humbug who simulates keenness in order to curry favour. And above all, he must make allowances for heredity and home influence. Many a Housemaster has been able to adjust his perspective with regard to a boy by remembering that the boy has a drunker father, or a neurotic mother, or no parents at all.

He must keep a light hand on House politics, knowing everything, yet doing little, and saying almost nothing at all. If a Housemaster be blatantly autocratic; if he deputes power to no one; if he prides himself upon his iron discipline; if he quells mere noise with savage ferocity and screws down the safety-valve implacably upon healthy ragging, he will reap his reward. He will render his House quiet, obedient – and furtive. Under such circumstances prefects are a positive danger. Possessing special privileges, but no sense of responsibility, they regard their office merely as a convenient and exclusive avenue to misdemeanour.

On the other hand, a Housemaster must not allow his prefects unlimited authority, or he will cease to be master in his own House. In other words, he must strike an even balance between sovereign and deputed power – an undertaking which has sent dynasties toppling before now.

In addition to all this, he must be an Admirable Crichton. Whatever his own particular teaching subject may be, he will be expected within the course of a single evening's "prep" to be able to unravel a knotty passage in Æschylus, "unseen", solve a quadratic equation on sight, compose a chemical formula, or complete an elegiac couplet. He must also be prepared at any hour of the day or night to explain how leg-breaks are manufactured, recommend a list of novels for the House library, set a broken collar-bone, solve a jig-saw puzzle in the Sickroom, assist an Old Boy in the choice of a career, or prepare a candidate for Confirmation. And the marvel is that he always does it – in addition to his ordinary day's work in the school.

And what is his remuneration? One of the rarest and most precious privileges that can be granted to an Englishman – the privilege of keeping a public house!

Let me explain. For the first twenty years of his professional career a schoolmaster works as a mere instructor of youth. By day he teaches his own particular subject; by night be looks over proses or corrects algebra papers. In his spare time he imparts private instruction to backward boys or scholarship candidates. Probably he bears a certain part in the supervision of the School games. He is possibly Treasurer of one or two of the boys' own organisations – the Fives Club or the Debating Society – and as a rule he is permitted to fill up odd moments by sub-editing the School magazine or organising sing-songs. He cannot as a rule afford to marry; so he lives the best years of his life in two rooms, looking forward to the time, in the dim and hypothetical future, when he will possess what the ordinary artisan usually acquires on passing out of his teens – a home of his own.

At length, after many days, provided that a sufficient number of colleagues die or get superannuated, comes his reward, and he enters upon the realisation of his dreams. He is now a Housemaster, with every opportunity (and full permission) to work himself to death.

Still, you say, the labourer is worthy of his hire. A man occupying a position so onerous and responsible as this will be well remunerated.

What is his actual salary?

In many cases, he receives no salary, as a Housemaster, at all. Instead, he is accorded the privilege of running his new home as a combined lodging-house and restaurant. His spare time (which the reader will have gathered is more than considerable) is now pleasantly occupied in purchasing beef and mutton and selling them to Binks tertius. As his tenure of the House seldom exceeds ten or fifteen years, he has to exercise considerable commercial enterprise in order to make a sufficient "pile" to retire upon – as Binks tertius sometimes discovers to his cost. In other words, a scholar and gentleman's reward for a life of unremitting labour in one of the most exacting yet altruistic fields in the world is a licence to enrich himself for a period of years by "cornering" the daily bread of the pupils in his charge. And yet we feel surprised, and hurt, and indignant when foreigners suggest that we are a nation of shopkeepers.

The life of a Housemaster is a living example of the lengths to which the British passion for undertaking heavy responsibilities and thankless tasks can be carried. Daily, hourly, he finds himself in contact (and occasional collision) with boys – boys for whose moral and physical welfare he is responsible; who in theory at least will regard him as their natural enemy; and who occupy the greater part of their leisure time in criticising and condemning him and everything that is his – his appearance, his character, his voice, his wife; the food that he provides and the raiment that he wears. He is harried by measles, mumps, servants, tradesmen and parents. He feels constrained to invite every boy in his House to a meal at least once a term, which means that he is almost daily deprived of the true-born Briton's birth-right of being uncommunicative at breakfast. His life is one long round of colourless routine, tempered by hair-bleaching emergencies.

But he loves it. He maintains, and ultimately comes to believe, that his House is the only House in the School in which both justice and liberty prevail, and his boys the only boys in the world who know the meaning of hard work, good food and *esprit de corps*. He pities all other Housemasters, and tells them so at frequent intervals; and he expostulates paternally and sorrowfully with form-masters who vilify the members of his cherished flock in half-term reports.

And his task is not altogether thankless. Just as the sun never sets upon the British Empire, so it never sets upon all the Old Boys of a great public school at once. They are gone out into all lands: they are upholding the honour of the School all the world over. And wherever they are – London, Simla, Johannesburg, Nairobi, or Little Pedlington Vicarage – they never lose touch with their old Housemaster. His correspondence is enormous; it weighs him down: but he would not relinquish a single picture postcard of it. He knows that wherever two or three of his Old Boys are gathered together, be it in Bangalore or Buluwayo, the talk will always drift round in time to the old School and the old House. They will refer to him by nickname – "Towser" or "Potbelly" or "Swiveleye" – and reminiscences will flow.

"Do you remember the old man's daily gibe when he found us chucking bread at dinner? 'Hah! There will be a bread pudding tomorrow!'"

"Do you remember the jaw he gave us when the news came about Macpherson's VC?"

"Do you remember his Sunday trousers? Oh, Lord!"

"Do you remember how he tanned Goat Hicks for calling The Frog a *cochon*? Fourteen, wasn't it?"

"Do you remember the grub he gave the whole House the time we won the House-match by one wicket, with Old Mike away?"

"Do you remember how he broke down at prayers the night little Martin died?"

"Do you remember his apologising to that young swine Sowerby before the whole House for losing his temper and clouting him over the head? That must have taken some doing. We rooted Sowerby afterwards for grinning."

"I always remember the time," interpolates one of the group, "when he scored me off for roller-skating on Sunday."

"How was that?"

"Well, it was this way. I had got leave of morning Chapel on some excuse or other, and was skating up and down the Long Corridor, having a grand time. The old man came out of his study – I thought he was in Chapel – and growled, looked at me over his spectacles – you remember the way?–"

"Yes, rather. Go on!"

"He growled:– 'Boy, do you consider roller-skating a Sunday pastime?' I, of course, looked a fool and said, 'No, sir.' 'Well,' chuckled the old bird, 'I do: but I always make a point of respecting a man's religious scruples. I will therefore confiscate your skates.' And he did! He gave them back to me next day, though."

"I always remember him," says another, "the time I nearly got sacked. By rights I ought to have been, but I believe he got me off at the last moment. Anyhow, he called me into his study and told me I wasn't to go after all. He didn't jaw me, but said I could take an hour off school and go and telegraph home that things were all right. My people had been having a pretty bad time over it, I knew, and so did he. I was pretty near blubbing, but I held out. Then, just as I got to the door, he called me back. I turned round, rather in a funk that the jaw was coming after all. But he growled out: -

"'It's a bit late in the term. The exchequer may be low. Here is sixpence for the telegram.'"

"This time I did blub. Not one man in a million would have thought of the sixpence. As a matter of fact, fourpence-halfpenny was all I had in the world."

And so on. His ears – especially his right ear – must be burning all day long.

Of course, all Housemasters are not like this. If you want to hear about the other sort, take up *The Lanchester Tradition*, by Mr. G. F. Bradby, and make the acquaintance of Mr. Chowdler – an individual example of a great type run to seed. And there is Dirty Dick, in *The Hill*.

• • • •

When he has fulfilled his allotted span as a Housemaster, our friend retires – not from school-mastering, but from the provision trade. With his hardly-won gains he builds himself a house in the neighbourhood of the school, and lives there in a state of *otium cum dignitate*. He still takes his form: he continues to do so until old age descends upon him, or a new broom at the head of affairs makes a clean sweep of the "permanent" staff.

He is mellower now. He no longer washes his hands of all responsibility for the methods of his colleagues, or thanks God that his boys are not as other masters' boys are. He does not altogether enjoy his work in school: he is getting a little deaf and is inclined to be testy. But teaching is his meat and his drink and his father and his mother. He sticks to it because it holds him to life.

Though elderly now, he enjoys many of the pleasures of middle age. For instance, he has usually married late, so his children are still young; and he is therefore spared the pain, which most parents have to suffer, of seeing the brood disperse just when it begins to be needed most. Or perhaps he has been too devoted to his world-wide family of boys to marry at all. In that case he lives alone; but you may be sure that his spare bedroom is seldom empty. No Old Boy ever comes home from abroad without paying a visit to his former Housemaster. Rich, poor, distinguished or obscure – they all come. They tell him of their adventures; they recall old days; they deplore the present condition of the School and the degeneracy of the Eleven; they fight their own battles over again. They confide in him their ambitions, and their failures – not their successes; those are for others to speak of – even their love affairs. And he listens to them all, and advises them all, this very tender and very wise old Ulysees. To him they are but boys still, and he would not have them otherwise.

"The heart of a Boy in the body of a Man," he says – "that is a combination which can never go wrong. If I have succeeded in effecting that combination in a single instance, then I have not run in vain, neither laboured in vain."

Chapter Three

SOME FORM-MASTERS

NUMBER ONE:
THE NOVICE

ARTHUR ROBINSON, BA, Late Exhibitioner of St. Crispin's College, Cambridge, having obtained a First Class, Division Three, in the Classical Tripos, came down from the University at the end of his third year and decided to devote his life to the instruction of youth.

In order to gratify this ambition as speedily as possible, he applied to a scholastic agency for an appointment. He was immediately furnished with type-written notices of some thirty or forty. Almost one and all, they were for schools which he had never heard of; but the post in every case was one which the Agency could unreservedly recommend. At the foot of each notice was typed a strongly worded appeal to him to write *(at once)* to the Headmaster, explaining first and foremost that he had *heard of this vacancy through our Agency*. After that he was to state his *degree (if any)*; *if a member of the Church of England*; *if willing to participate in School games*; *if musical*; and so on. He was advised, if he thought it desirable, to enclose a photograph of himself.

A further sheaf of such notices reached him every morning for about two months; but as none of them offered him more than a hundred-and-twenty pounds a year, and most of them a good deal less, Arthur Robinson, who was a sensible young man, resisted the temptation, overpowering to most of us, of seizing the very first opportunity of earning a salary, however small, simply because he had never earned anything before, and allowed the notices to accumulate upon one end of his mantelpiece.

Finally he had recourse to his old College tutor, who advised him of a vacancy at Eaglescliffe, a great public school in the west of England, and by a timely private note to the Headmaster secured his appointment.

Next morning Arthur Robinson received from the directorate of the scholastic agency – the existence of which he had almost forgotten – a rapturous letter of congratulations, reminding him that the Agency had sent him notice of the vacancy upon a specified date, and delicately intimating that their commission of five per cent upon the first year's salary was payable on appointment. Arthur, who had long since given up the task of breasting the Agency's morningtide of desirable vacancies, mournfully investigated the heap upon the mantelpiece, and found that the facts were as stated. There lay the notice, sandwiched between a document relating to the advantages to be derived from joining the staff of a private school in North Wales, where material prosperity was guaranteed by a salary of eighty pounds per annum, and social success by the prospect of meat-tea with the Principal and his family; and another, in which a clergyman (retired) required a thoughtful and energetic assistant (one hundred pounds a year, non-resident) to aid him in the management of a small but select seminary for backward and epileptic boys.

Arthur laid the matter before his tutor, who informed him that he must pay up, and be a little less casual in his habits in future. He therefore wrote a reluctant cheque for ten pounds, and having thus painfully imbibed the first lesson that a schoolmaster must learn – namely the importance of attending to details – departed to take up his appointment at Eaglescliffe.

He arrived the day before term began, to find that lodgings had been apportioned to him at a house in the village, half a mile from the School. He first evening was spent in making the place habitable. That is to say, he removed a number of portraits of his landlady's relatives from the walls and mantelpiece, and stored them, together with a collection of Early Victorian heirlooms – wool-mats and prism-laden glass vases – in a cupboard under the window-seat. In their place he set up fresh gods; innumerable signed photographs of young men, some in frames, some in rows along convenient ledges, others bunched together in a sort of wire entanglement much in vogue among the undergraduates of that time. Some of these photographs were mounted upon light blue mounts, and these were placed in the most conspicuous position. Upon the walls he hung a collection of framed groups of more young men, with bare knees and severe expressions, in some of which Arthur Robinson himself figured.

After that, having written to his mother and a girl in South Kensington, he walked up the hill in the darkness to the Schoolhouse, where he was to be received in audience by the Head.

The great man was sitting at ease before his study fire, and exhibited unmistakable signs of recent slumber.

"I want you to take Remove B, Robinson," he said. "They are a mixed lot. About a quarter of them are infant prodigies – Foundation Scholars – who make this form their starting-point for higher things; and the remainder are centenarians, who regard Remove B as a sort of scholastic Chelsea Hospital, and are fully prepared to end their days there. Stir 'em up, and don't let them intimidate the small boys into a low standard of work. Their subjects this term will be *Cicero de Senectute* and the *Alcestis*, without choruses. Have you any theories about the teaching of boys?"

"None whatever," replied Arthur Robinson frankly.

"Good! There is only one way to teach boys. Keep them in order: don't let them play the fool or go to sleep; and they will be so bored that they will work like niggers merely to pass the time. That's education in a nutshell. Good night!"

Next morning Arthur Robinson invested himself in an extremely new B.A. gown, which seemed very long and voluminous after the tattered and attenuated garment which he had worn at Cambridge – usually twisted into a muffler round his neck – and walked up to School. (It was the last time he ever walked thereafter, for many years, he left five minutes later, and ran.) Timidly he entered the Common Room. It was full of masters, some twenty or thirty of them, old, young, middle-aged. As many as possible were grouped round the fire – not in the orderly, elegant fashion of grown-up persons; but packed together right inside the fender, with their backs against the mantelpiece. Nearly everyone was talking and hardly anyone was listening to anyone else. Two or three – portentously solemn elderly men – were conferring darkly together in a corner. Others were sitting upon the table or arms of chairs, reading newspapers, mostly aloud. No one took the slightest notice of Arthur Robinson, who accordingly sidled into an unoccupied corner and embarked upon a self-conscious study of last term's time-table.

"I hear they have finished the new Squash Courts," announced a big man who was almost sitting upon the fire. "Take you on this afternoon, Jacker?"

"Have you got a court?" inquired the gentleman addressed.

"Not yet, but I will. Who is head of Games this term?"

"Etherington major, I think."

"Good Lord! He can hardly read or write, much less manage anything. I wonder why boys always make a point of electing congenital idiots to their responsible offices. Warwick, isn't old Etherington in your House?"

"He is," replied Warwick, looking up from a newspaper.

"Just tell him I want a Squash Court this afternoon, will you?"

"I am not a District Messenger Boy," replied Mr. Warwick coldly. Then he turned upon a colleague who was attempting to read his newspaper over his shoulder.

"Andrews," he said, "if you wish to read this newspaper I shall be happy to hand it over to you. If not, I shall be grateful if you will refrain from masticating your surplus breakfast in my right ear."

Mr. Andrews, scarlet with indignation, moved huffily away, and the conversation continued.

"I doubt if you will get a court, Dumaresq," said another voice – a mild one. "I asked for one after breakfast, and Etherington said they were all bagged."

"Well, I call that the limit!" bellowed that single-minded egotist, Mr. Dumaresq.

"After all," drawled a supercilious man sprawling across a chair, "the courts were built for the boys, weren't they?"

"They may have been built for the boys," retorted Dumaresq with heat, "but they were more than half paid for by the masters. So put that in your pipe, friend Wellings, and–"

"Your trousers are beginning to smoke," interpolated Wellings calmly. "You had better come out of the fender for a bit and let me in."

So the babble went on. To Arthur Robinson, still nervously perusing the time-table, it all sounded like an echo of the talk which had prevailed in the Pupil Room at his own school barely five years ago.

Presently, a fresh-faced elderly man crossed the room and tapped him on the shoulder.

"You must be Robinson," he said. "My name is Pollard, also of St. Crispin's. Come and dine with me tonight, and tell me how the old College is getting on."

The ice broken, the grateful Arthur was introduced to some of his colleagues, including the Olympian Dumaresq, the sarcastic Wellings, and the peppery Warwick. Next moment a bell began to ring upon the other side of the quadrangle, as there was a general move for the door.

Outside, Arthur Robinson encountered the Head.

"Good morning, Mr. Robinson!" (It was a little affectation of the Head's to address his colleagues as 'Mr.' when in cap and gown: at other times his key-note was informal bon-homie). "Have you your form-room key?"

"Yes, I have."

"In that case, I will introduce you to your flock."

At the end of the Cloisters, outside the locked door of Remove B, lounged some thirty young gentlemen. At the sight of the Head these ceased to lounge, and came to an attitude of uneasy attention.

The door being opened, all filed demurely in and took their seats, looking virtuously down their noses. The Head addressed the intensely respectable audience before him.

"This is Mr. Robinson," he said gruffly. "Do what you can for him."

He nodded abruptly to Robinson, and left the room.

As the door closed, the angel faces of Remove B relaxed.

"A-a-a-a-ah!" said everybody, with a sigh of intense relief.

Let us follow the example of the Head, and leave Arthur Robinson, for the present, to struggle in deep and unfathomed waters.

Number Two:
The Experts

Mr. Dumaresq was reputed to be the hardest slave-driver in Eaglescliffe. His eyes were cold and china blue, and his voice was like the neighing of a war-horse. He disapproved of the system of locked form-rooms – it wasted at least forty seconds, he said, getting the boys in – so he made his head boy keep the key and open the door the moment the clock struck.

Consequently, when upon this particular morning, Mr. Dumaresq stormed into his room, every boy was sitting at his desk.

"Greek prose scraps!" he roared, while still ten yards from the door.

Instantly each boy seized a sheet of school paper, and having torn it into four pieces selected one of the pieces and waited, pen in hand.

"*If you do this,*" announced Mr. Dumaresq truculently, as he swung into the doorway, "*you will be wise.*"

Every boy began to scribble madly.

"*If you do not do this,*" continued Mr. Dumaresq, "*you will not be wise. If you were to do this you would be wise. If you were not to do this you would not be wise. If you had done this you would have been wise. If you had not done this you would not have been wise.* Collect!"

The head boy sprang to his feet, and feverishly dragging the scraps from under the hands of his panting colleagues, laid them on the master's desk. Like lightning Mr. Dumaresq looked over them.

"Seven of you still ignorant of the construction of the simplest conditional sentence!" he bellowed. "Come in this afternoon!"

He tossed the papers back to the head boy. Seven of them bore blue crosses, indicating an error. There may have been more than one mistake in the paper, but one was always enough for Mr. Dumaresq.

"Now sit close!" he commanded.

"Sitting close" meant leaving comparatively comfortable and secluded desks, and crowding in a congested mass round the blackboard, in such wise that no eye could rove or mouth gape without instant detection.

"*Viva voce* Latin Elegiacs!" announced Mr. Dumaresq, with enormous enthusiasm. He declaimed the opening couplet of an English lyric. "Now throw that into Latin form. Adamson, I'm speaking to YOU! Don't sit mooning there, gaper. Think! Think!

Come lasses and lads, get leave of your dads–
Come on, man, come on!
–And away to the maypole, hey!

Say something! Wake up! How are you going to get over 'maypole'? No maypoles in Rome. Tell him, somebody! 'Saturnalia' – not bad. (Crabtree, stand up on the bench, and look at me, not your boots.) Why won't 'Saturnalia' do? Will it scan? *Think!* Come along, come *along!*"

In this fashion he hounded his dazed pupils through couplet after couplet, until the task as finished. Then, dashing at the blackboard, he obliterated the result of an hour's labour with a sweep of his duster.

"Now go to your desks, and write out a fair copy," he roared savagely.

So effective were Mr. Dumaresq's methods of inculcation that eighteen out his thirty boys succeeded in producing flawless fair copies. The residue were ferociously bidden to an "extra" after dinner. Mr. Dumaresq's "extras" were famous. He held at least one every day, not infrequently for the whole form. He possessed the one priceless attribute of the teacher: he never spared himself. Other masters would set impositions or give a boy the lesson to write out: Dumaresq, denying himself cricket or squash, would come into his form-room and wrestle with perspiring defaulters all during a hot afternoon until the task was well and truly done. Boys learned more from him in one term than from any other master in a year; but their days were but labour and sorrow. During the previous term a certain particularly backward member of his form had incurred some damage – to wit, a fractured collar-bone – during the course of a house-match. The pain was considerable, and when dragged from the scrimmage he was in a half-fainting condition. He revived as he was being carried to the Sanatorium.

"What's up?" he inquired mistily.

"Broken neck, inflammation of the lungs, ringworm, and leprosy, old son," announced one of his bearers promptly. "You are going to the San."

"Good egg!" replied the injured warrior. "I shall get off Dummy's extra after tea!"

Then, with a contented sigh, he returned to a state of coma.

• • • •

By way of contrast, Mr. Cayley.

As Mr. Cayley approached his form-room, which lay round a quiet corner, he was made aware of the presence of his pupils by sounds of turmoil; but being slightly deaf, took no particular note of the fact. Presently he found himself engulfed in a wave of boys, each of whom insisted upon shaking him by the hand. Some of them did so several times, but Mr. Cayley, whom increasing years had rendered a trifle dim-sighted, did not observe this. Cheerful greetings fell pleasantly but confusedly upon his ears.

"How do you do, sir? Welcome back to another term of labour, sir! Very well, no thank you! Stop shoving, there! Don't you see you are molesting Mr. Methuselah Cayley, MA? Permit me to open the door for you, sir! Now then, all together! Use your feet a bit more in the scrum!"

By this time the humorist of the party had possessed himself of the key of the door; but having previously stopped up the keyhole with paper, was experiencing some difficulty in inserting the key into the lock.

"Make haste, Woolley," said Mr. Cayley gently.

"I fear the porter has inserted some obstruction into the interstices of the aperture, sir," explained Master Woolley, in a loud and respectful voice. "He bungs up the hole in the holidays – to keep the bugs from getting in," he concluded less audibly.

"What was that, Woolley?" asked Mr. Cayley, thinking he had not heard aright.

Master Woolley entered with relish upon one of the standard pastimes of the Upper Fourth.

"I said some good tugs would get us in, sir," he replied, raising his voice and pulling paper out of the lock with a button hook.

Mr. Cayley, who knew that his ears were as untrustworthy as his eyes, but fondly imagined that his secret was his own, now entered his form-room upon the crest of a boisterous wave composed of his pupils, who, having deposited their preceptor upon his rostrum, settled down in their places with much rattling of desks and banging of books.

Mr. Cayley next proceeded to call for silence, and when he thought he had succeeded, said:

"As our new Latin subject books have not yet been distributed, I shall set you a short passage of unprepared translation this morning."

"Would it not be advisable, sir," suggested the head boy – the Upper Fourth addressed their master with a stilted and pedantic precocity of language which was an outrageous parody of his own courtly and old-fashioned utterance – "to take down our names and ages, as is usually your custom at the outset of your infernal havers?"

"Of what, Adams?"

"Of your termly labours, sir," said Adams, raising his voice courteously.

Mr. Cayley acquiesced in this proposal, and the form, putting their feet up on convenient ledges and producing refreshment from the secret recesses of their persons, proceeded to crack nuts and jokes, while their instructor laboured with studious politeness to extract from them information as to their initials and length of days. It was not too easy a task, for every boy in the room was conversing, and not necessarily with his next-door neighbour. Once a Liddell and Scott lexicon (medium size) hurtled through space and fell with a crash upon the floor.

Mr. Cayley looked up.

"Someone," he remarked with mild severity, "is throwing India-rubber."

Name-taking finished, he made another attempt to revert to the passage of unprepared translation. But a small boy, with appealing eyes and a wistful expression, rose from his seat and timidly deposited a large and unclean object upon Mr. Cayley's desk.

"I excavated this during the holidays, sir," he explained; "and thinking it would interest you, I made a point of preserving it for your inspection."

Instant silence fell upon the form. Skilfully handled, this new diversion was good for quite half an hour's waste of time.

"This is hardly the moment, Benton," replied Mr. Cayley, "for a disquisition on geology, but I appreciate your kindness in thinking of me. I will examine this specimen this afternoon, and classify it for you."

But Master Benton had no intention of permitting this.

"Does it belong to the glacial period, sir?" he inquired shyly. "I thought these marks might have been caused by ice-pressure."

There was a faint chuckle at the back of the room. It proceeded from the gentleman whose knife Benton had borrowed ten minutes before in order to furnish support for his glacial theory.

"It is impossible for me to say without my magnifying-glass," replied Mr. Cayley, peering myopically at the stone. "But from a cursory inspection I should imagine this particular specimen to be of an igneous nature. Where did you get it?"

"In the neck!" volunteered a voice.

Master Benton, whose cervical vertebræ the stone had nearly severed in the course of a friendly interchange of missiles with a playmate while walking up to school, hastened to cover the interruption.

"Among the Champion Pills, sir," he announced gravely.

"The Grampian Hills?" said Mr. Cayley, greatly interested. He nodded his head. "That may be so. Geologically speaking, some of these hills were volcanoes yesterday."

"There was nothing about it in the *Daily Mail* this morning," objected a voice from the back benches.

"I beg your pardon?" said Mr. Cayley, looking up.

"It sounds like a fairytale sir," amended the speaker.

"And so it is!" exclaimed Mr. Cayley, the geologist in him aroused at last. "The whole history of nature is a fairytale. Cast your minds back for a thousand centuries…"

The form accepted this invitation to the extent of dismissing the passage of unprepared translation from their thoughts for ever, and settling down with a grateful sigh, began to search their pockets for fresh provender. The seraph-like Benton slipped back into his seat. His mission was accomplished. The rest of the hour was provided for.

Three times in the past five years Mr. Cayley's colleagues had offered to present him with a testimonial. He could never understand why.

• • • •

Mr. Bull was a young master, and an international football player. Being one of the few members of the staff at Eaglescliffe who did not possess a first-class degree, he had been entrusted with the care of the most difficult form in the school – the small boys, usually known as The Nippers.

A small boy is as different from a middle-sized boy as chalk from cheese. He possesses none of the latter's curious dignity and self-consciousness. He has the instincts of the puppy, and appreciates being treated as such. That is to say, he is physically incapable of sitting still for more than fifteen minutes at a time; he is never happy except in the company of a drove of other small boys; and he is infinitely more amenable to the *fortiter in re* than to the *suaviter in modo* where the enforcement of discipline is concerned. Above all, he would rather have his head smacked than be ignored.

Mr. Bull greeted his chattering flock with a hearty roar of salutation, coupled with a brisk command to them to get into their places and be quick about it. He was answered by a shrill and squeaky chorus, and having thrown open the form-room door herded the whole swarm within; assisting stragglers with a genial cuff or two; which, coming from so great a hero, were duly cherished by their recipients as marks of special favour.

Having duly posted up the names and tender ages of his Nippers in his mark-book, Mr. Bull announced :

"Now we must appoint the Cabinet Ministers for the term."

Instantly there came a piping chorus.

"Please, sir, can I be Scavenger?"

"Please, sir, can I be Obliterator?"

"Please, sir, can I be Window-opener?"

"Please, sir, can I be Inkslinger?"

"Please, sir, can I be Coalheaver?"

"Shut up!" roared Mr. Bull, and the babble was quelled instantly. "We will draw lots as usual."

Lots were duly cast, and the names of the fortunate announced. Mr. Bull was not a great scholar: some of the "highbrow" members of the Staff professed to despise his humble attainments. But he understood the mind of extreme youth. Tell a small boy to pick up waste-paper, or fill an inkpot, or clean a blackboard, and he will perform these acts of drudgery with natural reluctance and shirk them when he can. But appoint him Lord High Scavenger, or Lord High Inkslinger, or Lord High Obliterator, with sole right to perform these important duties and power to eject usurpers, and he will value and guard his privileges with all the earnestness and tenacity of a permanent official.

Having arranged his executive staff to his satisfaction, Mr. Bull announced:–

"We'll do a little English literature this morning, and start fair on ordinary work this afternoon. Sit absolutely still for ten minutes while I read to you. Listen all the time, for I shall question you when I have finished. After that you shall question me – one question each, and mind it is a sensible one. After that, a breather; then you will write out in your own words a summary of what I have read. Atten*shun*!"

He read a hundred lines or so of *The Passing of Arthur*, while the Nippers, restraining itching hands and feet, sat motionless. Then followed question time, which was a lively affair; for questions mean marks, and Nippers will sell their souls for marks. Suddenly, Mr. Bull shut the book with a snap.

"Out you get!" he said. "The usual run – round the Founders Oak and straight back. And no yelling, mind! Remember, there are others." He took out his watch. "I give you one minute. Any boy taking longer will receive five thousand lines and a public flogging. Off!"

There was a sudden upheaval, a scuttle of feet, and then solitude.

The last Nipper returned panting, with his lungs full of oxygen and the fidgets shaken out of him, within fifty-seven seconds, and the work of the hour proceeded.

• • • •

Each master had his own method of maintaining discipline. Mr. Wellings, for instance, ruled entirely by the lash of his tongue. A schoolboy can put up with stripes, and he rather relishes abuse; but sarcasm withers him to the marrow. In this respect Mr. Wellings' reputation throughout the school – he was senior mathematical master, and almost half the boys passed through his hands – was that of a "chronic blister".

Newcomers to his sets, who had hitherto regarded the baiting of subject-masters as a mild form of mental recuperation between two bouts of the Classics, sometimes overlooked this fact. If they had a reputation for lawlessness to keep up they sometimes endeavoured to make themselves obnoxious. They had short shrift.

"Let me see," Wellings would drawl, "I am afraid I can't recall your name for the moment. Have you a visiting card about you?"

Here the initiated would chuckle with anticipatory relish, and the offender, a little taken aback, would either glare defiantly or efface himself behind his book.

"I am addressing you, sir – you in the back bench, with the intelligent countenance and the black-edged finger-nails," Wellings would continue in silky tones. "I asked you a question just now. Have you a visiting card about you?"

A thousand brilliant repartees would flash through the brain of the obstreperous one. But somehow, in Wellings' mild and apologetic presence, they all seemed either irrelevant or fatuous. He usually ended by growling, "No."

"Then what is your name – or possibly title? Forgive me for not knowing."

"Corbett." It is extraordinary how ridiculous one's surname always sounds when one is compelled to announce it in public.

"Thank you. Will you kindly stand up, Mr. Corbett, in order that we may study you in greater detail?" (Mr. Wellings had an uncanny knack of enlisting the rest of the form on his side when he dealt with an offender of this type.) "I must apologise for not having heard of you before. Indeed, it is surprising that one of your remarkable appearance should hitherto have escaped my notice in my walks abroad. The world knows nothing of its greatest men: how true that it! However, this is no time for moralising. What I wanted to bring to your distinguished notice is this – that you must not behave like a yahoo in my mathematical set. During the past ten minutes you have kicked one of your neighbours and cuffed another: you have partaken of a good deal of unwholesome and (as it came out of your pocket) probably unclean refreshment; and you have indulged in several childish and obscene gestures. These daredevil exploits took place while I was writing on the blackboard: but I think it only fair to mention to you that I have eyes in the back of my head – a fact upon which any member of this set could have enlightened you. But possibly they do not presume to address a person of your eminence. I have no idea, of course, with what class of society you are accustomed to mingle; but here – *here* – that sort of thing is simply not done, really! I am so sorry! But the hour will soon be over, and then you can go and have a nice game of shove-halfpenny, or whatever your favourite sport is, in the gutter. But at present I must ask you to curb your natural instincts. That is all, thank you very much. You may sit down now. Observe from time to time the demeanour of your companions, and endeavour to learn from them. They do not possess your natural advantages in the way of brains and beauty, but their manners are better. Let us now resume our studies."

Mr. Wellings used to wonder plaintively in the Common Room why his colleagues found it necessary to set so many impositions.

•   •   •   •

Lastly, Mr. Klotz. Mr. Klotz may be described as a Teutonic survival – a survival of the days when it was *de rigueur* to have the French language taught by a foreigner of some kind. Not necessarily by a Frenchman – that would have been pandering too slavishly to Continental idiosyncrasy – but at least by some one who could only speak broken English. Mr. Klotz was a Prussian, so possessed all the necessary qualifications.

His disciplinary methods were modelled upon those of the Prussian Army, of which he had been a distinguished ornament – a fact of which he was fond of reminding his pupils, and which had long been regarded by those guileless infants as one of the most valuable weapons in their armoury of time-wasting devices.

Mr. Klotz, not being a resident master, had no special classroom or key: he merely visited each form-room in turn. He expected to find every boy in his seat ready for work upon his arrival; and as he was accustomed to enforce his decrees at the point of the bayonet – or its scholastic equivalent – sharp scouts and reliable sentries were invariably posted to herald his approach.

Behold him this particular morning marching into Remove A form-room, which was situated at the top of a block of buildings on the south side of the quadrangle, with the superb assurance and grace of a Prussian subaltern entering a beer-hall.

Having reached his desk, Mr. Klotz addressed his pupils.

"He who rount the corner looked when op the stairs I game," he announced, "efter lonch goms he!"

The form, some of them still breathless from their interrupted rag, merely looked down their noses with an air of seraphic piety.

"Who was de boy who did dat?" pursued Mr. Klotz.

No reply.

"Efter lonch," trumpeted Mr. Klotz, "goms eferypoty!"

At once a boy rose in his place. His name was Tomlinson.

"It was me, sir," he said.

"Efter lonch," announced Mr. Klotz, slightly disappointed at being robbed of a holocaust, "goms Tomleenson. I gif him irrecular verps."

Two other boys rose promptly to their feet. Their names were Pringle and Grant. They had not actually given the alarm, but they had passed it on.

"It was me, too, sir," said each.

"Efter lonch," amended Mr. Klotz, "goms Tomleenson, Brinkle unt Grunt. Now I take your names unt aitches."

This task accomplished, Mr. Klotz was upon the point of taking up *Chardenal's First French Course*, when a small boy with a winning manner (which he wisely reserved for his dealings with masters) said politely:–

"Won't you tell us about the Battle of Sedan, sir, as this is the first day of term?"

The bait was graciously accepted, and for the next hour Mr. Klotz ranged over the historic battle-field. It appeared that he had been personally responsible for the success of the Prussian arms, and had been warmly thanked for his services by the Emperor, Moltke, and Bismarck.

"You liddle Engleesh boys," he concluded, "you think your Army is great. In my gontry it would be noding – noding! Take it away! Vat battles has it fought to compare–"

The answer came red-hot from thirty British throats:

"Waterloo!" (There was no "sir" this time.)

"Vaterloo?" replied Mr. Klotz condescendingly. "Yes. But vere would your Engleesh army haf been at Vaterlook without Blucher?" He puffed out his chest. "Tell me dat, Brinkle!"

"Blucher, sir?" replied Master Pringle deferentially. "Who was he, sir?"

"You haf not heard of Blucher?" gasped Mr. Klotz in genuine horror.

The form, who seldom encountered Mr. Klotz without hearing of Blucher, shook their heads with polite regret. Suddenly a hand shot up. It was the hand of Master Tomlinson, who it will be remembered had already burned his boats for the afternoon.

"Do you mean Blutcher, sir?" he inquired.

"Blutcher? Himmel! Nein!" roared Mr. Klotz. "I mean Blucher."

"I expect he was the same person, sir," said Tomlinson soothingly. "I remember him now. He was the Russian who–"

"Prussian!" yelled the infuriated Mr. Klotz.

"I beg your pardon, sir – Prussian. I thought they were the same thing. He was the Prussian general whom Lord Wellington was relying on to back him up at Waterloo. But Blutcher – Blucher lost his way – quite by accident, of course – and did not reach the field until the fight was over."

"He stopped to capture a brewery, sir, didn't he?" queried Master Pringle, coming to his intrepid colleague's assistance.

"It was bad luck his arriving late," added Tomlinson, firing his last cartridge; "but he managed to kill quite a lot of wounded.

Mr. Klotz had only one retort for enterprises of this kind. He rose stertorously to his feet, crossed the room, and grasping Master Tomlinson by the ears, lifted him from his seat and set him to stand in the middle of the floor. Then he returned for Pringle.

"You stay dere," he announced to the pair, "ontil the hour is op. Efter lonch–"

But in his peregrinations over the battle-field of Sedan, Mr. Klotz had taken no note of the flight of time. Even as he spoke, the clock struck.

"The hour is up now, sir!" yelled the delighted form.

And they dispersed with tumult, congratulating Pringle and Tomlinson upon their pluck and themselves upon a most profitable morning.

But it is a far cry to Sedan nowadays. The race of Klotzes has perished, and their place is occupied by muscular young Britons who have no reminiscences and whose pronunciation, both of English and German, is easier to understand.

Chapter Four

BOYS

NUMBER ONE:
THE GOVERNMENT

"THERE'S YOUR journey money, Jackson. Good-bye, and a pleasant holiday!"

"Thank you, sir. The same to you!" replies Jackson dutifully.

They shake hands, and the Housemaster adds:–

"By the way, I shall want you to join the prefects next term."

"Me, sir? Oh!"

"Yes. Endeavour to get accustomed to the idea during the holidays. It will make a big difference in your life here. I am not referring merely to sausages for tea. Try and think out all that it implies."

Then follows a brief homily. Jackson knows it by heart, for it never varies, and he has heard it quoted frequently, usually for the purposes of derision.

"The prefect in a public-school occupies the same position as the non-commissioned officer in the Army. He is promoted from the ranks; he enjoys privileges not available to his former associates; and he is made responsible to those above him not merely for his own good behaviour but for that of others. Just as it would be impossible to run an army without non-commissioned officers, so it would be impossible, under modern conditions, to run a public school without prefects."

Jackson shifts his feet uneasily, after the immemorial fashion of schoolboys undergoing a "jaw".

"But I want to warn you of one or two things," continues the wise old Housemaster.

Jackson looks up quickly. This part of the exhortation is new. At least, he has never heard it quoted.

"You will have certain privileges: don't abuse them. You will have certain responsibilities: don't shirk them. And above all, don't endeavour to run with the hare and hunt with the hounds. You will be strongly tempted to do so. Your old associates will regard you with suspicion – even distrust; and that will sting. In your anxiety to show to them that your promotion has not impaired your capacity for friendship, you may be inclined to stretch the Law in their favour from time to time, or even ignore it altogether. On the other hand, you must be aware of over-officiousness towards those who are not your friends. A little authority is a dangerous thing. So walk warily at first. That's all. Good night, old man."

• • • •

They shook hands again, and Jackson returned soberly to his study, which he shared with his friend Blake. The two had entered the School the same day: they had fought their way up side by side from its lowest walks to a position of comparative eminence; and their friendship, though it contained no David and Jonathan elements – very few schoolboy friendships do – had survived the severe test of two years study-companionship. Jackson was the better scholar, Blake the better athlete of the two. Now, one was taken and the other left.

Blake, cramming miscellaneous possessions into his grub-box in view of the early departure on the morrow, looked up.

"Hallo!" he remarked. "You've been a long time getting your journey-money. Did the old Man try to cut you down?"

"No... He says I'm to be a prefect next term."

"Oh! Congratters!" said Blake awkwardly.

"Thanks. Has he made you one too?" asked Jackson.

"No."

"Oh. What rot!"

Presently Jackson's oldest friend, after an unhappy silence, rose and went out. He had gone to join the proletariat round the Hall fire. The worst of getting up in the world is that you have to leave so many old comrades behind you. And worse still, the comrades frequently persist in believing that you are glad to do so.

Such is the cloak of Authority, as it feels to a thoughtful and sensitive boy who assumes it for the first time.

Of course, there are others. Hulkins, for instance. In his eyes the prefectorial system was created for his express convenience and glorification. He opens the study door and bawls:

"Fa-a-a-ag!"

A dozen come running. The last to arrive is bidden to remove Hulkin's boots from his feet and bring slippers. The residue have barely returned to their noisy fireside when Hulkins' voice is uplifted again. This time he requires blotting-paper, and the last comer in the panting crowd is sent into the next study to purloin some. The rest have hardly regained their fastness when there is a third disturbance, and there is Hulkins howling like a lost soul for matches. And so, with infinite uproar and waste of labour, the great man's wants are supplied. It does the fags no harm, but it is very, very bad for Hulkins.

Frisby is another type. He is not afraid of assuming responsibility. He is a typical new broom. He dots the i's and crosses the t's of all the tiresome little regulations in the House. He sets impositions to small boys with great profusion, and sees to it that they are shown up punctually. If it is his turn to take roll-call, he descends to the unsportsmanlike device of waiting upon the very threshold of the Hall until the clock strikes, and then coming in and shutting the door with a triumphant bang in the faces of those who had reckoned on the usual thirty seconds' grace. He ferrets out the misdemeanours of criminals of fourteen, and gibbets them. He is terribly efficient – but his vigilance and zeal stop suddenly short at the prospect of a collision with any malefactor more than five feet high.

Then there is Meakin. He receives his prefectship with a sigh of relief. For four years he has led a hunted and precarious existence in the lower walks of the House. His high-spirited playmates have made him a target for missiles, derided his style of running, broken his spectacles, raided his study, wrecked his collection of beetles, and derived unfailing joy from his fluent but impotent imprecations. Now, at last, he sees peace ahead. He will be left to himself, at any rate. They will not dare to rag a prefect unless the prefect endeavours to exert his authority unduly, and Meakin has no intention whatever of doing that. To Frisby, Office is a sharp two-edged sword: to Meakin, it is merely a shield and buckler.

Then there is Flabb. He finds a prefect's lot a very tolerable one. He fully appreciates the fleshpots in the prefect's room; and he feels that it is pleasant to have fags to whiten his cricket-boots and make toast for his tea. He maintains friendly relations with the rest of the House, and treats small boys kindly. He performs his mechanical duties – roll-call, supervision of Prep, and the like – with as little friction as possible. But he does not go out of his way to quell riots or put down bullying; and when any unpleasantness arises between the Prefects and the House, Flabb effaces himself as completely as possible.

Finally, there is Manby, the head of the House. He is high up in the Sixth, and a good all-round athlete. He weighs twelve stone ten, and fears nothing – except a slow ball which comes with the bowler's arm. To him government comes easily. The House hangs upon his lightest word, and his lieutenants go about the business with assurance and despatch. He is a born organiser and a natural disciplinarian. His prestige overawes the unofficial aristocracy of the House – always the most difficult section. And he stands no nonsense. A Manby of my acquaintance once came upon twenty-two young gentlemen in a corner of the cricket-field, who, having privily abandoned the orthodox game arranged for their benefit that afternoon, were indulging in a pleasant but demoralising pastime known as "tip-and-run". Manby, addressing them as "slack little swine, a disgrace to the House", chastised them one by one, and next half-holiday made them play tip-and-run under a broiling sun and his personal supervision from two o'clock till six.

A House with a Manby at the head of it is safe. It can even survive a weak Housemaster. Greater Britain is run almost entirely by Manbys.

Taking it all round, the prefectorial machine works well. It is by no means perfect, but it is infinitely more efficient than any other machine. The chief bar to its smooth running is the inherent loyalty of boys to one another and their dislike of anything which savours of tale-bearing. Schoolboys have no love for those who go out of their way to support the arm of the Law, and a prefect naturally shrinks from being branded as a master's jackal. Hence, that ideal – a perfect understanding between a Housemaster and his prefects – is seldom achieved. What usually happens is that when the Housemaster is autocratically inclined he runs the House himself, while the prefects are mere lay figures; and when the Housemaster is weak or indolent the prefects take the law into their own hands and run the House, often extremely efficiently, with as little reference to their titular head as possible. He is a great Housemaster who can co-operate closely with his prefects without causing friction between the prefects and the House, or the prefects and himself.

But sometimes an intolerable strain is thrown upon the machine – or rather, upon the most sensitive portions of it.

Look at this boy, standing uneasily at the door of his study, with is fingers upon the handle. Outside, in the passage, a riot is in progress. It is only an ordinary exuberant "rag": he himself has participated in many such. But the Law enjoins that his particular passage shall be kept perfectly quiet between the hours of eight and nine in the evening; and it is this boy's particular duty, as the only prefect resident in the passage, to put the Law into effect.

He stands in the darkness of his study, nerving himself. The crowd outside numbers ten or twelve; but he is not in the least afraid of that. This enterprise calls for a different kind of courage, and a good deal of it. Jackson is not a particularly prominent member of the House, except by reason of his office: others far more distinguished than himself are actually participating in the disturbance outside. It will be of no avail to emerge wrathfully and say: "Less row, there!" He said that three nights ago. Two nights ago he said it again, and threatened reprisals. Last night he named various offenders by name, and stated that if the offence was repeated he would report them to the Housemaster. *Tonight he has got to do it.* The revellers outside know this: the present turmoil is practically a challenge. To crown all, he can hear above the din, in the very forefront of battle, the voice of Blake, once his own familiar friend.

With Blake Jackson had reasoned privily only that afternoon, warning him that the House would go to pot if its untitled aristocracy took to inciting others, less noble, to deeds of lawlessness. Blake had replied by recommending his late crony to return to his study and boil his head. And here he was, leading tonight's riot.

What will young Jackson do? Watch him well, for from his action now you will be able to forecast the whole of his future life.

He may remain mutely in his study, stop his ears, and allow the storm to blow itself out. He may appear before the roysterers and utter vain repetitions, thereby salving his conscience without saving his face. Or he may go out like man and fulfil his promise of last night. It sounds simple enough on paper. But consider what it means to a boy of seventeen, possessing no sense of perspective to tone down the magnitude of the disaster he is courting. Jackson hesitates. Then, suddenly:

"I'll be *damned* if I take it lying down!" he mutters.

He draws a deep breath, turns the handle, and steps out. Next moment he is standing in the centre of a silent and surly ring, jotting down names.

"You five," he announces to a party of comparatively youthful offenders, "can come to the prefect's room after prayers and be tanned. You three" – he indicates the incredulous Blake and two surly satellites – "will have to be reported. I'm sorry, but I gave you fair warning last night."

He turns on his heel and departs in good order to his study, branded – for life, he feels convinced – as an officious busybody, a presumptuous upstart, and worst of all, a betrayer of old friends. He has of his own free will cast himself into the nethermost Hell of the schoolboy – unpopularity – all to keep his word.

And yet for acts of mere physical courage they give men the Victoria Cross.

NUMBER TWO:
THE OPPOSITION

TO CONDUCT the affairs of a nation requires both a Government and an Opposition. So it is with school politics. The only difference is that the scholastic Opposition is much franker about its true aims.

The average schoolboy, contemplating the elaborate arrangements made by those in authority for protecting him from himself – rules, roll-calls, bounds, lock-ups, magisterial discipline and prefectorial supervision – decides that the ordering and management of the school can be maintained without any active assistance from him; and he plunges joyously into Opposition with all the abandon of a good sportsman who knows that the odds are heavily against him. He breaks the Law, or is broken by the Law, with equal cheerfulness.

The most powerful member of the Opposition is the big boy who has not been made a prefect, and is not likely to be made a prefect. He enjoys many privileges – some of them quite unauthorised – and has no responsibilities. He is one of the happiest people in the world. He has reached the age and status at which corporal punishment is supposed to be too degrading to be feasible: this immunity causes him to realise that he is a personage of some importance; and when he is addressed rudely by junior form-masters he frequently stands upon his dignity and speaks to his Housemaster about it. His position in the House depends firstly upon his athletic ability, and secondly upon the calibre of the prefects. Given a timid set of prefects, and an unquestioned reputation in the football world, Master Bullock has an extremely pleasant time of it. He possesses no fags, but that does not worry him. I once knew a potentate of this breed who improvised a small gong out of the lid of a biscuit tin, which he hung in his study. When he beat upon this with a tea-spoon, all within earshot were expected to (and did) come running for orders. Such as refrained were chastised with a toasting-fork.

Then comes a great company of which the House recks nothing, and of whom the House history has little to tell – the Cave-Dwellers, the Swots, the Smugs, the Saps. These keep within their own lurking places, sedulously avoiding the noisy conclaves which crowd sociably round the Hall fire. For one thing, the conversation there bores them intensely, and for another they would seldom be permitted to join in it. The *rôle* of Sir Oracle is strictly confined to the athletes of the House, though the Wag and the Oldest Inhabitant are usually permitted to offer observations or swell the chorus. But the Cave-Dwellers, never.

The curious part about it is that not by any means all the Cave-Dwellers are "Swots". It is popularly supposed that any boy who exhibits a preference for the privacy of his study devotes slavish attention therein to the evening's Prep, thus stealing a march upon his more sociable and less self-centred brethren. But this is far from being the case. Many of the Cave-Dwellers dwell in caves because they find it more pleasant to read novels, or write letters, or develop photographs, or even do nothing, than listen to stale House gossip or indulge in everlasting small cricket in a corridor.

They are often the salt of the House, but they have no conception of the fact. They entertain a low opinion of themselves: they never expect to rise to any great position in the world: so they philosophically follow their own bent, and leave the glory and the praise to the athletes and their *umbræ*. It comes as quite a shock to many of them, when they leave school and emerge into a larger world, to find themselves not only liked but looked up to; while the heroes of their schooldays, despite their hairy arms and club ties, are now dismissed in a word as "hobble-de-hoys."

Then comes the Super-Intellectual – the "Highbrow". He is a fish out of the water with a vengeance, but he does exist at school – somehow. He congregates in places of refuge with others of the faith; and they discuss the *English Review*, and mysterious individuals who are only referred to by their initials – as G.B.S. and G.K.C. Sometimes he initiates these discussions because they really interest him, but more often, it is to be feared, because they make him feel superior and grown-up. Somewhere in the school grounds certain youthful schoolmates of his, inspired by precisely similar motives but with different methods of procedure, are sitting in the centre of a rhododendron bush smoking cigarettes. In each case the idea is the same – namely, a hankering after meats which are not for babes. But the smoker puts on no side about his achievements, whereas the "highbrow" does. He loathes the vulgar herd and holds it aloof. He does not inform the vulgar herd of this fact, but he confides it to the other highbrows, and they applaud his discrimination. Intellectual snobbery is a rare thing among boys, and therefore difficult to account for. Perhaps the pose is a form of reaction. It is comforting, for instance, after you have been compelled to dance the can-can in your pyjamas for the delectation of the Lower Dormitory, to foregather next morning with a few kindred spirits and discourse pityingly and scathingly upon the gross philistinism of the lower middle classes.

No, the lot of the æsthete at school is not altogether a happy one, but possibly his tribulations are not without a certain beneficent effect. When he goes up to Oxford or Cambridge he will speedily find that in the tolerant atmosphere of those intellectual centres the prig is not merely permitted to walk the earth but to flourish like the green bay-tree. Under the intoxicating effects of this discovery the recollection of the robust and primitive traditions of his old School – and the old School's method of instilling those traditions – may have a sobering and steadying effect upon him. No man ever developed his mind by neglecting his body, and if the memory of a coarse and ruthless school tradition can persuade the Super-Intellectual to play hockey or go down to the river after lunch, instead of sitting indoors drinking liqueurs and discussing Maupassant with a coterie of the elect, then the can-can in the Lower Dormitory has not been danced altogether in vain.

Then come the rank and file. There are many types. There is the precocious type, marked out for favourable notice by aptitude at games and attractive manners. Such a one stands in danger of being taken up by older boys than himself; which means that he will suffer the fate of all those who stray out of their proper station. At first he will be an object of envy and dislike; later, when his patrons have passed on elsewhere, he may find himself friendless.

At the opposite end of the scale comes the Butt. His life is a hard one, but not without it compensations; for although he is the target of all the practical humour in the House, his post carries with it a certain celebrity; and at any rate a Butt can never be unpopular. So he is safe at least from the worst disaster that can befall a schoolboy. Besides, you require a good deal of character to be a Butt.

And there is the Buffoon. He is distinct from the Butt, because a Butt is usually a Butt *malgré lui*, owing to some peculiarity of appearance or temperament; whereas the Buffoon is one of those people who yearn for notice at any price, and will sell their souls "to make fellows laugh." You may behold him, the centre of a grinning group, tormenting some shy or awkward boy – very often the Butt himself; while in school he is the bugbear of weak masters. The larger his audience the more exuberant he becomes: he reaches his zenith at a breaking-up supper or in the back benches on Speech Day. One is tempted to feel that when reduced to his own society he must suffer severely from depression.

Then there is the Man of the World. He is a recognised authority on fast life in London and Bohemian revels in Paris. He is a patron of the drama, and a perfect mine of unreliable information as to the private life of the originals of the dazzling portraits which line his study – and indeed half the studies in the House. The picture-postcard, as an educative and refining influence, has left an abiding mark upon the youth of the present day. We of an older and more rugged civilisation, who were young at a period when actresses' photographs cost two shillings each, were compelled in those days to restrict our gallery of divinities to one or two at the most. (Too often our collection was second-hand, knocked down for sixpence at some end-of-term auction, or reluctantly yielded in composition for a long-outstanding debt by a friend in the throes of a financial crisis.) But nowadays, with the entire Gaiety chorus at a penny apiece, the youthful connoisseur of female beauty has emancipated himself from the pictorial monogamy (or at the most, bigamy) of an earlier generation. He is a polygamist, a pantheist. He can erect an entire feminine Olympus upon his mantelpiece for the sum of half-a-crown. And yet, bless him, he is just as unsophisticated as we used to be – no more and no less. The type does not change.

Lastly, comes the little boy – the Squeaker, the Tadpole, the Nipper, what you will. His chief characteristic is terrific but short-lived enthusiasm for everything he undertakes, be it work, play, a friendship, or a private vendetta.

He begins by taking education very seriously. He is immensely proud of his first set of books, and writes his name on nearly every page, accompanied by metrical warnings to intending purloiners. He equips himself with a perfect arsenal of fountain-pens, rubber stamps, blue pencils, and ink-erasers. He starts a private mark-book of his own, to check possible carelessness or dishonesty on the part of his form-master. Then he gets to work, with his books disposed around him and his fountain-pen playing all over his manuscript. By the end of a fortnight he has lost all his books, and having broken his fountain-pen, is detected in a pathetic attempt to write his exercise upon a sheet of borrowed paper with a rusty nib held in his fingers or stuck into a splinter from off the floor.

It is the same with games. Set a company of small boys to play cricket, and their solemnity at the start is almost painful. Return in half an hour, and you will find that the stately contest has resolved itself into a reproduction of the parrot-house at the Zoo, the point at issue being a doubtful decision of the umpire's. Under the somewhat confiding arrangement which obtains in Lower School cricket, the umpire for the moment is the gentleman whose turn it is to bat next; so litigation is frequent. Screams of "Get out!" "Stay in!" "Cads!" "Liars!" rend the air, until a big boy or a master strolls over and quells the riot.

The small boy's friendships, too, are of a violent but ephemeral nature. But his outstanding characteristic is a passion for organising secret societies of the most desperate and mysterious character, all of which come speedily to a violent or humiliating dissolution.

I was once privileged to be introduced into the inner workings of a society called "The Anarchists". It was not a very original title, but it served its time, for the days of the Society were few and evil. Its aims were sanguinary and nebulous; the Rules consisted almost entirely of a list of the penalties to be inflicted upon those who transgressed them. For instance, under Rule XXIV any one who broke Rule XVII was compelled to sit down for five minutes upon a chair into the seat of which a pot of jam had been emptied. (Economists will be relieved to hear that the jam was afterwards eaten by the executioners, the criminal being very properly barred from participating.)

The Anarchists had a private code of signals with which to communicate with one another in the presence of outsiders – in Prep, for instance. The code was simplicity itself. A single tap with a pencil upon the table denoted the letter A; two taps B; and so on. As may be imagined Y and Z involved much mental strain; and as the transmitter of the message invariably lost count after fourteen or fifteen taps, and began all over again without any attempt either at explanation or apology, the gentleman who was acting as receiver usually found the task of decoding his signals a matter of extreme difficulty and some exasperation. Before the tangle could be straightened out a prefect inevitably swooped down and awarded both signallers fifty lines for creating a disturbance in Preparation.

However, the Anarchists, though they finished after the manner of their kind, did not slip into oblivion so noiselessly as some of their predecessors. In fact, nothing in their inky and jabbering life became them like their leaving of it.

One evening the entire brotherhood – there were about seven of them – were assembled in a study which would have held four comfortably, engaged in passing a vote of censure upon one Horace Bull, B.A., their form-master. Little though he knew it, Bull had been a marked man for some weeks. The Czar of all the Russias himself could hardly have occupied a more prominent position in the black books of Anarchy in general. Today he had taken a step nearer his doom by clouting one Nixon minor, Vice-President of the Anarchists, on the side of the head.

It was during the geography hour. Mr. Bull had asked Nixon to define a watershed. Nixon, who upon the previous evening had been too much occupied with his duties as Vice-President of the Anarchists to do much Prep, had replied with a seraphic smile that a watershed was "a place to shelter from the rain". As an improvised effort the answer seemed to him an extremely good one; but Mr. Bull had promptly left his seat, addressed Nixon as a "cheeky little hound", and committed the assault complained of.

"This sort of thing," observed Rumford tertius, the President, "can't go on. What shall we do?"

"We might saw one of the legs of his chair through," suggested one of the members.

"Who's going to do it?" inquired the President. "We'll only get slain."

Silence fell, as it usually does when the question of belling the cat arrives at the practical stage.

"We could report him to the Head," said another voice. "We might get him the sack for assault – even quod! We could show Nixon's head to him. It would be a sound scheme to make it bleed a bit before we took him up."

The speaker fingered a heavy ruler lovingly, but Mr. Nixon edged coldly out of reach.

"Certainly," agreed the President, "Bashan ought to be stopped knocking us about in form."

"I'd rather have one clout over the earhole," observed an Anarchist who so far had not spoken, "than to be taken along to Bashan's study and given six of the best. That is what the result would be. Hallo, Stinker, what's that?"

The gentleman addressed – a morose, unclean, and spectacled youth of scientific proclivities – was the latest recruit to the gang. He had been admitted at the instance of Master Nixon, who had pointed out that it would be good thing to enrol as a member someone who understood "Chemistry and Stinks generally". He could be used for the manufacture of bombs, and so on.

Stinker had produced from his pocket a corked test-tube, tightly packed with some dark substance.

"What's that?" inquired the Anarchists in chorus. (They nearly always talked in chorus.)

"It's a new kind of explosive," replied the inventor with great pride.

"I hope it's better than that new kind of stinkpot you invented for choir-practice," remarked a cynic from the corner of the study. "That was a rotten fraud, if you like! It smelt more like lily-of-the-valley than any decent stink."

"Dry up, Ashley minor!" rejoined the inventor indignantly. "This is a jolly good bomb. I made it today in the Lab, while The Badger was trying to put out a bonfire at the other end."

"Where does the patent come in?" inquired the President judicially.

"The patent is that it doesn't go off all at once."

"We know *that!*" observed the unbelieving Ashley.

"Do you chuck it or light it?" asked Nixon.

"You light it. At least, you shove it into the fire, and it goes off in about ten minutes. You see the idea? If Bashan doesn't see us put anything into the form-room fire, he will think it was something wrong with the coal."

The Anarchists, much interested, murmured approval.

"Good egg!" observed the President. "We'll put it into the fire tomorrow morning before he comes in, and after we have been at work ten minutes or so the thing will go off and blow the whole place to smithereens."

"Golly!" gobbled the Anarchists.

"What about us, Stinker?" inquired a cautious conspirator. "Shan't we get damaged?"

Stinker waved away the objection.

"We shall know it's coming," he said, "so we shall be able to dodge it. But it will be a nasty jar for Bashan."

There was a silence, full of rapt contemplation of tomorrow morning. Then the discordant voice of Ashley minor broke in.

"I don't believe it will work. All your inventions are putrid, Stinker."

"I'll fight you!" squealed the outraged scientist, bounding to his feet.

"I expect it'll turn out to be a fire-extinguisher, or something like that," pursued the truculent Ashley.

"Hold the bomb," said Stinker to the President, "while I–"

"Sit down," urged the other Anarchists, drawing in their toes. "There's no room here. Ashley minor, chuck it!"

"It won't work," mutter Ashley doggedly.

Suddenly a brilliant idea came upon Stinker.

"Wont' work, won't it?" he screamed. "All right, then! We'll shove it into this fire now, and you see if it doesn't work!"

Among properly constituted Anarchistic Societies it is not customary, when the efficacy of a bomb is in dispute, to employ the members as a *corpus vile*. But the young do not fetter themselves with red-tape of this kind. With one accord Stinker's suggestion was acclaimed, and the bomb was thrust into the glowing coals of Rumford's study fire. The brotherhood, herded together within a few feet of the grate – the apartment measured seven feet by six – breathed hard and waited expectantly.

Five minutes passed – then ten.

"It ought to be pretty ripe now," said the inventor anxiously.

The President, who was sitting next to the window, prudently muffled his features in the curtain. The others drew back as far as they could. – about six inches – and waited.

Nothing happened.

"I am sure it will work all right," declared the inventor desperately. "Perhaps the temperature of this fire—"

He knelt down, and began to blow upon the flickering coals. There was a long and triumphant sniff from Ashley.

"I said it was only a rotten stinkp—" he began.

BANG!

There is a special department of Providence which watches over the youthful chemist. The explosion killed no one, though it blew the coals out of the grate and the pictures off the walls.

The person who suffered most was the inventor. He was led, howling but triumphant, to the Sanatorium.

"Luckily, sir," explained Rumford to Mr. Bull a few days later, in answer to a kindly enquiry as to the extent of the patient's injuries, "it was only his face."

Chapter Five

THE PURSUIT OF KNOWLEDGE

I

ONE OF the most pathetic spectacles in the world is that of grown-up persons legislating for the young. Listening to these, we are led to suspect that a certain section of the human race – the legislative section – must have been born into the world aged about forty, sublimely ignorant of the requirements, limitations and point of view of infancy and adolescence.

In what attitude does the ordinary educational expert approach educational problems? This question induces another. What is an educational expert?

The answer is simple. Practically everybody.

All parents are educational experts: we have only to listen to a new boy's mother laying down to a Headmaster the lines upon which his school should be conducted to realise that. So are all politicians: we discover this fact by following the debates in the House of Commons. So are the clergy; for they themselves have told us so. So, presumably, are the writers of manuals and text-books. So are the dear old gentlemen who come down to present prizes upon Speech Day. Practically the only section of humanity to whom the title is denied are the people who have to teach. It is universally admitted by the experts – it is their sole point of agreement – that no schoolmaster is capable of forming a correct judgment of the educational needs of his charges. He is hidebound, "groovy"; he cannot break away from tradition. "What can you expect from a tripe-dresser," inquire the experts in chorus, "but a eulogy of the stereotyped method of dressing tripe?"

So, ignoring the teacher, the experts lay their heads – one had almost said their loggerheads – together, and evolve terrific schemes of education. Each section sets out its task in characteristic fashion. The politician, with his natural acumen, gets down to essentials at once.

"The electorate of this country," he says to himself, "do not care one farthing dip about Education as such. Now, how can we galvanise Education into a vote-catching machine?"

He reflects.

"Ah! I have it!" he cries presently. "*Religion!* That'll ginger them up!"

So presently an Education Bill is introduced into the House of Commons. Nine out of its ten clauses deal purely with educational matters and are passed without a division; and the intellectual teeth of the House fasten greedily upon Clause Number Ten, which deals with the half-hour per day which is to be set aside for religious instruction. The question arises: What attitude are the youth of the country to be taught to adopt towards their Maker? Are they to praise Him from a printed page, or merely listen to their teacher doing so out of his own head? Are they to learn the Catechism? Is the Lord's Prayer to be regarded as an Anglican or Non-conformist orison?

Everybody is most conciliatory at first.

"A short passage of Scripture," suggest the Anglicans; "a Collect, mayhap; and a few words of helpful instruction – eh? Something quite simple and non-contentious, like that?"

"We are afraid that that is sectarian religion," object the Non-conformists. "A simple chapter from the Bible, certainly – may be a hymn. But no dogmatic teaching, *if* you please!"

"But that is no religion at all!" explain the Anglicans, with that quickness to appreciate another's point of view which has always distinguished the Church of England.

After a little further unpleasantness all round, a deadlock is reached. Then, with that magnificent instinct for compromise which characterises British statesmanship, another suggestion is put forward. Why not permit all the clergy of the various denominations to enter the School and minister to the requirements of their various young disciples? "An admirable notion", says everybody. But difficulties arise. Are this heavenly host to be admitted one by one, or in a body? If the former, how long will it take to work through the entire rota, and when will the ordinary work of the day be expected to begin? If the latter, is the School to be divided, for devotional purposes, into spiritual water-tight compartments by an arrangement of movable screens, or what? So the battle goes on. By this time, as the astute politician has foreseen, every one has forgotten that this is an Education Bill, and both sides are hard at work manufacturing party capital out of John Bull's religious susceptibilities. Presently the venue is shifted to the country, where the electorate are asked upon a thousand platforms if the Church which inaugurated Education in our land, and built most of the schools, is to be ousted from her ancient sphere of beneficent activity; and upon a thousand more, whether the will of the People or the Peers is to prevail. (It simplifies politics very greatly to select a good reliable shibboleth and employ it on *all* occasions.) Finally the Bill is thrown out or talked out, and the first nine clauses perish with it.

That is the political and clerical way of dealing with Education. The parent's way we will set forth in another place.

The writer of manuals and text-books concerns himself chiefly with the right method of unfolding his subject to the eager eyes of the expectant pupil. "There is a right way and a wrong way," he is careful to explain; "and if you present your subject in the wrong way the pupil will derive no *educational* benefit from it whatever. At present there is a great craze for what is known as "practical" teaching. For instance, in our youth we were informed, *ad nauseam*, that there is a certain fixed relation between the circumference of a circle and its diameter, the relation being expressed by a mysterious Greek symbol pronounced "pie". The modern expert scouts this system altogether. No imaginary pie for him! He is a practical man.

Take several ordinary tin canisters, he commands, a piece of string, and a ruler; and without any other aids ascertain the circumference and diameters of these canisters. Work out in each case the numerical relation between the circumference and diameter. What conclusion do you draw from the result?

We can only draw one, and that is that no man who has never been a boy should be permitted to write books of instruction for the young. For what would he "result" be? Imagine a company of some thirty or forty healthy happy boys, each supplied gratuitously with several tin canisters and a ruler, set down for the space of an hour and practically challenged to create a riot. Alexander's Rag-Time Band would be simply nowhere!

As for the last gang of experts – the dear old gentlemen who come down to give away prizes on Speech Day – they do not differ much as a class. They invariably begin by expressing a wish that they had enjoyed such educational facilities as these in their young days.

"You live in a palace, boys!" announces the old gentleman. "I envy you." (Murmurs of "Liar!" from the very back row.)

After that the speaker communicates to his audience a discovery which has been communicated to the same audience by different speakers since the foundation of the School – to this effect, that Education (derivation given here, with a false quantity thrown in) is a "drawing out" and not a "putting-in". Why this fact should so greatly excite Speech Day orators is not known, but they seldom fail to proclaim it with intense and parental enthusiasm. Then, after a few apposite remarks upon the subject of *mens sana in corpore sano* – a flight of originality received with murmurs of anguish by his experienced young hearers – the old gentleman concludes with a word of comfort to "the less successful scholars". It is a physical impossibility, he points out, when there is only one prize, for all the boys in the class to win it; and adds that his experience of life has been that not every boy who wins prizes at school becomes Prime Minister in after years. All of which is very helpful and illuminating, but does not solve the problem of Education to any great extent.

So much for the experts. Their name is Legion, for they are many, and they speak with various and dissonant voices. But they have one thing in common. All their schemes of education are founded upon the same amazing fallacy – namely, that a British schoolboy is a person who desires to be instructed. That is the rock upon which they all split. That is why it was suggested earlier in these pages that educational experts are all born grown-up.

Let us clear our minds upon this point once and for all. In nine cases out of ten a schoolmaster's task is not to bring light to the path of an eager, groping disciple, but to drag a reluctant and refractory young animal up the slopes of Parnassus by the scruff of his neck. The schoolboy's point of view is perfectly reasonable and intelligible. "I am lazy and scatter-brained," he says in effect. "I have not as yet developed the power of concentration, and I have no love of knowledge for its own sake. Still, I have no rooted objection to education, as such, and I suppose I must learn something in order to earn a living. But I am much too busy, as a growing animal, to have any energy left for intellectual enterprise. It is the business of my teacher to teach me. To put the matter coarsely, he is paid for it. I shall not offer him effusive assistance in his labours, but if he succeeds in keeping me up to the collar against my will, I shall respect him for it. If he does not, I shall take full advantage of the circumstance."

That is the immemorial attitude of the growing boy. When he stops growing, conscience and character begin to develop, and he works because he feels he ought to or because he has got into the habit of doing so, and not merely because he must. But until he reaches that age it is foolish to frame theories of education based upon the idea that a boy is a person anxious to be educated.

Let us see how such a theory works, say, in the School laboratory. A system which will extract successful results from a class of boys engaged in practical chemistry will stand any test we care to apply to it. Successful supervision of School science is the most ticklish business that a master can be called upon to undertake. We will follow our friend Brown minor to the laboratory and witness him at his labours.

He takes his place at the working bench, and sets out his apparatus – test-tubes, beakers, and crucibles. He lights all the Bunsen burners within reach. Presently he is provided with a sample of some crystalline substance and bidden to ascertain its chemical composition.

"How shall I begin, sir? he asks respectfully.

"Apply the usual tests: I told you about them yesterday in the lecture-room. Take small portions of the substance: ascertain if they are soluble. Observe their effect on litmus. Test them with acid, and note whether a gas is evolved. And so on. That will keep you going for the present. I'll come round to you again presently."

And off goes the busy master to help another young scientist in distress.

Brown minor gets to work. He takes a portion of the crystalline substance and heats it red-hot, in the hope that it will explode; and treats another with concentrated sulphuric acid in order to stimulate it into some interesting performance. At the same time he maintains a running fire of *sotto voce* conversation and chaff with his neighbours – a laboratory offers opportunities for social intercourse undreamed of in a form-room – and occasionally leaves his own task in order to assist, or more often to impede, the labours of another. When he returns to his place he not infrequently finds that his last decoction (containing the balance of the crystalline substance) has boiled over, and is now lying in a simmering pool upon the bench, or that another chemist has called and appropriated the vessel in which the experiment was proceeding, emptying its contents down the sink. Not a whit disturbed, he fills up the time with some work of independent research, such as the manufacture of a Roman candle or the preparation of a sample of nitro-glycerine. At the end of the hour he reports progress to his instructor, expressing polite regret at having failed as yet to solve the riddle of the crystalline substance; and returns whistling to his form-room where he jeers at those of his companions who have spent the morning composing Latin verses.

No, it is a mistake to imagine that the young of the human animal hungers and thirsts after knowledge.

Arthur Robinson, B.A., of whom previous mention has been made, soon discovered this fact; or rather, soon recognised it; for he was not much more than a boy himself. He was an observant and efficient young man, and presently he made further discoveries.

The first was that boys, for teaching purposes, can be divided into three classes:

(A) Boys whose conduct is uniformly good, and whose industry is continuous. Say fifteen per cent.

For example, Master Mole. He was invariably punctual; his work was always well prepared; and he endured a good deal of what toilers in another walk of life term "peaceful picketing" for contravening one of the fundamental laws of schoolboy trades-unionism by continuing to work when the master was out of the room.

(B) Boys whose conduct is uniformly good – except perhaps in the matter of surreptitious refreshment – but who will only work so long as they are watched. Say sixty per cent.

Such a one was Master Gibbs. By long practice he had acquired the art of looking supremely alert and attentive when in reality his thoughts were at the back of beyond. When engaged in writing work his pen would move across the page with mechanical regularity, what time both eyes were fixed upon a page torn from a comic paper and secreted under his manuscript. He gave no trouble whatever, but was a thorn in the flesh of any conscientious teacher.

(C) Boys who are not only idle, but mischievous. Say twenty-five per cent.

There was Page, whose special line was the composition of comic answers to questions. Some of his efforts were really praiseworthy; but like all adventurous spirits he went too far at last. The rod descended upon the day when he translated *cæruleæ puppes* "Skye terriers"; and thereafter Master Page joked no more. But it was a privation for both boy and master.

Then there was Chugleigh, whose strong suit was losing books. He was a vigorous and muscular youth, more than a little suspected of being a bully; but he appeared to be quite incapable of protecting his own property. Sometimes he grew quite pathetic about it. He gave Mr. Robinson to understand, almost with tears, that his books were at the mercy of any small boy who cared to snatch them from him. Certainly he never had any in form.

"I see you require State protection," said Arthur Robinson one morning when Chugleigh put in an appearance without a single book of any kind, charged with a rambling legend about his locker and a thief in the night. He scribbled an order. "Take this to the librarian, and get a new set of books."

Mr. Chugleigh, much gratified – the new books would be paid for by an unsuspicious parent and could be sold second-hand at the end of the term – departed, presently to return with new five volumes under his arm.

"Write your name in them all," said Mr. Robinson briskly.

Chugleigh obeyed, as slowly as possible.

"Now bring all the books here."

Chugleigh did so, a little puzzled.

"For the future," announced Mr. Robinson, unmasking his batteries, "in order to give you a fair chance in this dishonest world, you shall have *two* sets of the books in use in this form. I will keep one set for you. The others you may keep or lose as you like, but whenever you turn up here without a book I shall be happy to hire you out the necessary duplicate, at a charge of threepence per book per hour. This morning you will require a Cæsar, a grammar, and a Latin Prose book. That will be ninepence. Will you pay cash, or shall I knock it off your pocket money at the end of the week?"

He locked up the remaining two books in his desk, and the demoralised Chugleigh resumed his seat amid loud laughter.

II

The pursuit of knowledge, like the pursuit of other precious things in life, occasionally leads its votaries into tortuous ways. Cribbing, for instance.

All boys crib more or less. It is not suggested that the more sinful forms of this species of self-help are universal, or even common. But the milder variations are practised by all, with the possible exception of the virtuous fifteen per cent, previously mentioned.

The average boy's attitude towards cribbing is precisely the same as his attitude towards other types of misdemeanour: that is to say, he regards it as one of these things which is perfectly justifiable if his form-master is such a weakling as to permit it. It is all part of the eternal duel between the teacher and the taught.

"Do I scribble English words in the margin of my Xenophon?" asks the boy. "Certainly. Do I surreptitiously produce loose pages of Euclid from my pocket and copy them out, when I am really supposed to have learned them by heart? Of course. Why should I, through sheer excess of virtue, handicap myself in the race to escape the punishment of failure, simply because the highly qualified expert who is paid to supervise my movements fails in his plain duty?"

So he cribs.

But his attitude towards the matter is quite consistent, for when he rises to a position of trust and authority in the school, he ceases to crib – at least flagrantly. The reason is that he is responsible now not so much to a master as to his own sense of right and wrong; and he has made the discovery which all of us make in the end – that the little finger of our conscience is often thicker than the hardest taskmaster's loins.

There are two forms of cribbing, and the school opinion differentiates very sharply between them. There is cribbing to gain marks and there is cribbing to save trouble or avoid punishment. The average boy, who is in the main an honest individual, holds aloof from the former practice because he feels that it is unsportsmanlike – rather like stealing, in fact; but he usually acquiesces without a struggle in the conveniences offered by the second. For instance, he refrains from furtively copying from his neighbour, for he regards that as the meanest kind of brain-sucking. (If the neighbour pushes his paper towards him with a friendly smile, that of course is a different matter.) But he is greatly addicted to a more venial crime known as "paving". The paver prepares his translation in the orthodox manner, but whenever he has occasion to look up a word in a lexicon he scribbles its meaning in the margin of the text, or, more frequently, just over the word itself, to guard against loss of memory on the morrow.

Much less common is the actual use of cribs – the publications of the eminent house of Bohn, and other firms of less reliability and repute. Most boys have sufficient honesty and common sense to realise that getting up work with a translation is an unprofitable business, though at the same time they are often unable to resist the attractions of such labour-saving appliances. Their excuse is always the same, and it is not a bad one.

"If the School Library," they say, "contains Jowett's Thucydides and Jebb's Sophocles for all the Sixth to consult, why should not we, in our humbler walk of scholarship, avail ourselves of the occasional assistance of Kiddem's Keys to the Classics?"

So much for the casual cribber. The professional – the chronic – exercises an ingenuity, and devotes an amount of time and labour to the perfecting of his craft which, if applied directly to his allotted task, would bring him out at the top of his form. In a little periodical entitled *The Light Green*, published in Cambridge thirty years ago by a young Johnian named Hilton (who might have rivalled Calverley himself had he lived to maturity), we have a brilliant little portrait of the professional cribber, executed in the style of *The Heathen Chinee*. It is called *The Heathen Passee*.

> In the crown of his cap
> Were the Furies and Fates,
> And an elegant map
> Of the Dorian States:
> And we found in his palms, which were hollow,
> What are common in palms – that is dates.

But he is a rare bird, the confirmed cribber, with his algebraical formulæ written on his finger-nails, and history notes attached to unreliable elastic arrangements which shoot up his sleeve out of reach at critical moments. The ordinary boy does not crib unless he is pressed for time or in danger of summary execution. He usually limits his enterprises to co-operative preparation – that is to say, the splitting up an evening's work into sections, each section being prepared by one boy and translated to the other members of the syndicate afterwards – to the gleaning of discarded lines and superfluous tags from the rough copies of cleverer boys' Latin Verses, and to the acceptance of a whispered "prompt" from a good Samaritan when badly cornered by a question.

But we may note that cribbing is not confined to schoolboys. The full perfection of the art is only attained in the pass-examinations of the

Universities of Oxford and Cambridge. Then all considerations of conscience or sportsmanship are flung aside, and the cribber cribs, not to gain distinction or outstrip his rivals, but to get over a troublesome fence by hook or by crook and have done with it. There was once a Freshman at Cambridge whose name began with M. This accident of nomenclature placed him during his Little Go examination in the next seat to a burly young man whom he recognised with a thrill of awe as the President of the C.U.B.C., whose devotion to aquatic sports had so far prevented him from clearing the academic fence just mentioned, and who now, at the beginning of his third year, was entering, in company with a collection of pink-faced youths fresh from school, upon his ninth attempt to satisfy the examiners in Part One of the Previous Examination.

Our friend, having completed his first paper, quitted the Senate House and returned to his rooms, to fortify himself with luncheon before the next. During the progress of that meal a strange gyp called upon him, and proffered a note, mysteriously.

"From Mr. M— sir," he said, mentioning the name of the Freshman's exalted neighbour in the examination room.

The Freshman opened the note with trembling fingers. Was it possible that he had been singled out as a likely oar already?

• • • •

The note was brief, but to the point. It said:
"Dere Sir,
Please write larger.
Yours truly,
J.M—."

III

However, this is a digression. Let us return for the last time to Arthur Robinson's three divisions of youthful humanity. Class A he found extraordinarily dull. They required little instruction and no supervision; in fact, they were self-educators of the most automatic type. Class B were a perpetual weariness to the flesh. They gave no trouble, but their apathy was appalling. However, a certain amount of entertainment could be extracted from studying their methods of evading work or supplying themselves with refreshment. There was the ingenious device of Master Jobling, for instance. Mr. Robinson noted that this youth was in the habit, during lecture-time, of sitting with his elbows resting on his desk and his chin buried in his hands, his mouth, or a corner thereof, being covered by his fingers. His attitude was one of rapt attention, and his eyes were fixed unwinkingly upon the lecturer. Such virtue, coming from Master Jobling, roused unworthy suspicions in the breast of Arthur Robinson. He observed that although the youth's attitude was one of rigid immobility, his facial muscles were agitated from time to time by a slight convulsive movement. Accordingly, one day, he stepped swiftly across the room, and taking Master Jobling by the hair, demanded an explanation. It was forthcoming immediately, in the form of a long thin India-rubber tube, of the baby's bottle variety; one end of which was held between Master Jobling's teeth, while the other communicated, *via* his right sleeve, with a bottle of ginger-beer secreted somewhere in the recesses of his person. From this reservoir he had been refreshing himself from time to time by a process of suction.

Mr. Robinson, who believed in making the punishment fit the crime, purchased a baby's "soother" from the chemist's, and condemned Jobling to put it to its rightful use during every school-hour for the rest of the week. He was only allowed to remove it from his lips in order to answer a question.

Class C, the professional malefactors, Mr. Robinson found extremely attractive. They appeared to possess all the character and quite half the brains of the form. But this is a permanent characteristic of the malefactor, and is most discouraging to the virtuous.

Once early in his career, Robinson was badly caught. On entering his form-room one winter evening, when darkness had fallen and the gas was ablaze, his eye fell upon the great plate-glass window which filled the south wall of the room. Form-room windows are not usually supplied with blinds, and this window stood black and opaque against the darkness of the night. Right in the centre of the glass was a great white star, which radiated out in all directions in a series of splintered cracks.

Mr. Robinson knew well what had happened. Someone had hurled a stone inkpot against the window. Only last week he had had occasion to discourage target-practice of this kind by exemplary measures. He addressed the crowded form angrily.

"Who broke that window?"

"It is not broken, sir," volunteered a polite voice.

Arthur Robinson was a young man who did not suffer impudence readily.

"This is not precisely the moment," he rapped out, "for nice distinctions. The window is cracked, starred, splintered – anything you like. I want the name of the boy who damaged it. At once, please!"

Silence. Yet it was not the sullen, obstinate silence which prevails when boys are endeavouring to screen one another. One would almost have called it silent satisfaction. But Arthur Robinson was too angry and not sufficiently experienced to note the distinction. Naming each boy by name, he demanded of him whether or not he had broken the window. Each boy politely denied the impeachment. One or two were courteous to the point of patronage.

Suddenly, from the back bench, came a faint chuckle. Arthur Robinson, conscious of a sickly feeling down his spine, rose to his feet and approached the splintered window. The form watched him with breathless joy. Hot faced, he rubbed one of the rays of the star with his fingers. It promptly disappeared.

The window was undamaged. The star was artistically executed in white chalk.

Malefactors have their weak spots, too.

One afternoon Mr. Robinson held an "extra". That is to say, he brought in a body of sinful youths, composed of the riff-raff of his form, for a period of detention and set them a stiff imposition to write out. About half-way through the weary hour he produced from his locked desk an old cigarette box containing sundry coins. Laying these out before him, he proceeded to count them. The perfunctory scratching of pens ceased, and the assembled company, most of whom had been unwilling contributors to the fund under review, gazed with lack-lustre eyes at their late property.

"Fourteen-and-nine," announced Mr. Robinson cheerfully. "That is the sum which I have collected from you this term in return for the loan of such useful articles as pens and blotting-paper. I know my charges are high; but then I am a monopolist to people who are foolish enough to come in here without their proper equipment. Again, though threepence may seem a fancy price for a small piece of blotting-paper, it is better to pay threepence for a piece of blotting-paper than use your handkerchief, which is worth a shilling. However, the total is fourteen-and-nine. What shall we do with it? Christmas is only a fortnight off, and I propose, with your approval, to send this contribution of yours to a society which provides Christmas dinners for people who are less lavishly provided for in that respect than ourselves. If it interests you at all, I will get the Society's full title and address and read them to you."

Arthur Robinson was out of the room for perhaps three minutes. When he returned he was immediately conscious, from the guilty stillness which reigned, and the self-conscious air of detachment with which everybody was writing, that something was amiss. He glanced sharply at the little pile of money on his desk.

It had grown from fourteen-and-ninepence to twenty-seven-and-sixpence.

Life is full of compensations – even for schoolmasters.

Chapter Six

SCHOOL STORIES

ONE OF the most striking features of the present day cult of The Child is the fact that whereas school stories were formerly written to be read by schoolboys, they are now written to be read – and are read with avidity – by grown-up persons.

This revolution has produced some abiding results. In the first place, school stories are much better written than they were. Secondly, a certain proportion of the limelight has been shifted from the boy to the master, with the result that school life is now presented in a more true and corporate manner. Thirdly, school stories have become less romantic, less sentimental, more coldly psychological. They are tinged with adult worldliness, and, too often, with adult pessimism. As literature they are an enormous advance upon their predecessors; but what they have gained in *savoir faire* they appear to have lost in *joie de vivre*.

Let us enter upon the ever-fascinating task of comparing the old with the new.

To represent the ancients we will take that immortal giant, *Tom Brown*. With him, as they say in legal circles, *Eric*. Many people will say, and they will be right, that Tom Brown would make a much braver show for the old brigade if put forward alone, minus his depressing companion. But we must bear in mind that it takes more than one book to represent a literary era. We will therefore call upon Tom Brown and Eric Williams between them to represent the schoolboy of a bygone age.

Most of us make Tom Brown's acquaintance in early youth. We fortify ourselves with a course of him before going to school for the first time- at the age of twelve or thereabout – and we quickly realise, even at that tender age, that there were giants in those days.

Have you ever considered Tom Brown's first day at school? No? Then observe. He was called at half-past two in the morning, at the Peacock

Inn, Islington, and by three o'clock was off as an "outside" upon the Tally-Ho Coach, in the small hours of a November morning, on an eighty-mile drive to Rugby.

He arrived at his destination just in time to take dinner in Hall, chaperoned by his new friend East; and then, *duce* Old Brooke, plunged into that historic football match between the Schoolhouse and the School – sixty on one side and two hundred on the other. Modern gladiators who consider "two thirty-fives" a pretty stiff period of play will be interested to note that this battle raged for three hours, and that the Schoolhouse were filled with surprise and rapture at achieving a goal after only sixty minutes' play. ("A goal in an hour! Such a thing had not been done in a Schoolhouse match these five years.")

In the course of the game, Tom was knocked over while stopping a rush, and as the result of spending some minutes at the bottom of a heap of humanity composed of a goodly proportion of his two hundred opponents, was finally hauled out "a motionless body". However, he recovered sufficiently to be able to entertain East to tea and sausages in the Lower Fifth School. After a brief interval for ablution came supper, followed by a free-and-easy musical entertainment in the Schoolhouse hall, which included singing, a good deal of indiscriminate beer-drinking, and the famous speech of Old Brooke. Tom, it is hardly necessary to say, obliged with a song – "with much applause".

Then came prayers, and Tom's first glimpse of the mighty Arnold. (We may note here that a new boy of the old days was not apparently troubled by tiresome regulations upon the subject of reporting himself to his housemaster on arrival.) Even then Tom's first day from home was not over, for before retiring to his slumber he was tossed in a blanket three times. Not a bad record for a boy of twelve! And yet we flatter ourselves that we live a strenuous life.

Customs have changed in many respects since Tom Brown's time. Public schoolboys of eighteen or nineteen do not now wear beards, neither do they carry pea-shooters. Our athletes array themselves for battle in the shortest of shorts and the thinnest of jerseys. The participators of the three-hour Schoolhouse match merely took off their jackets and hung them upon the railings or trees. We are told, however, with some pride, that those who meant *real* work added their hats, waistcoats, neck-handkerchiefs, and braces! What of those who did not? Again, a captain does not nowadays "administer toco" upon the field of battle to subordinates who have failed to prevent the enemy from scoring a try. Again, no master of today would dare to admit to a boy that he "does not understand" cricket, or for that matter draw parallels between cricket and Aristophanes for the benefit of an attentive audience in a corner of the playing-field during a school match.

But we all accept all these incidents in *Tom Brown* without question. We never dream of doubting that they occurred, or could have occurred. Arthur, we admit, is a rare bird, but he is credible. Even East's religious difficulties, or rather his anxiety to discuss them, are made convincing. The reason is that *Tom Brown* contains nothing that is alien from human nature – schoolboy human nature. It is the real thing all through. Across the ages, Tom Brown of Rugby speaks to Brown minor (also, possibly, of Rugby) with the voice of a brother. Details may have changed, but the essentials are the same. "How different," we say, "but oh, how like!"

Not so at all times with *Eric, or Little by Little*. Here we miss the robust philistinism of the eternal schoolboy, and the atmosphere of reality which pervades *Tom Brown*. We feel that we are not *living* a story, but merely reading it. *Eric* does not ring true. We suspect the reverend author – to employ an expression which his hero would never have used – of "talking through his hat".

None of us desire to scoff at true piety or moral loftiness, but we feel instinctively that in *Eric* these virtues are somewhat indecently paraded. The schoolboy is essentially a matter-of-fact animal, and extremely reticent. He is not usually concerned with the state of his soul, and never under any circumstances anxious to discuss the matter; and above all he abhors the preacher and the prig. *Eric, or Little by Little* is priggish from start to finish. Compare, for instance, Eric's father and Squire Brown. Here are the Squire's meditations as to the advice he should give Tom before saying good-bye:

"I won't tell him to read his Bible, and love and serve God; if he don't do that for his mother's sake and teaching, he won't for mine. Shall I go into the sort of temptations he'll meet with? No, I can't do that. Never do for an old fellow to go into such things with a boy. He won't understand me. Do him more harm than good, ten to one. Shall I tell him to mind his work, and say he's sent to school to make himself a good scholar? Well, but he isn't sent to school for that – at any rate, not for that mainly. I don't care a straw for Greek particles, or the digamma; no more does his mother. What is he sent to school for? Well, partly because he wanted so to go. If he'll only turn out a brave, helpful, truth-telling Englishman, and a gentleman, and a Christian, that's all I want."

Now compare Eric's father in one of his public appearances. That worthy but tiresome gentleman suddenly descends upon the bully Barker, engaged in chastising Eric.

"There had been an unobserved spectator of the whole scene, in the person of Mr. Williams himself, and it was his strong hand that now gripped Barker's shoulder. He was greatly respected by the boys, who all knew his tall handsome figure by sight, and he frequently stood a quiet and pleased observer of their games. The boys in the playground came crowding round, and Barker in vain struggled to escape. Mr. Williams held him firmly, and said in a calm voice, 'I have just seen you treat one of your schoolfellows with the grossest violence. It makes me blush for you, Roslyn boys,' he continued, turning to the group that surrounded him, 'that you can even for a moment stand by unmoved, and see such things done. Now; mark; it makes no difference that the boy who has been hurt is my own son; I would have punished this scoundrel whoever it had been, and I shall punish him now.' With these words, he lifted the riding-whip which he happened to be carrying, and gave Barker by far the severest castigation he had ever undergone. He belaboured him till his sullen obstinacy gave way to a roar for mercy, and promises never so to offend again.

"At this crisis he flung the boy from him with a 'phew' of disgusts, and said, 'I give nothing for your word; but if ever you do bully in this way again, and I see or hear of it, your present punishment shall be a trifle to what I shall then administer. At present, thank me for not informing your master.' So saying, he made Barker pick up the cap and, turning away, walked home with Eric leaning on his arm."

Poor Eric! What chance can a boy have had whose egregious parent insisted upon outraging every canon of schoolboy law on his behalf? We are not altogether surprised to read, a little later, that though from that day Eric was never troubled with personal violence from Barker, "rancour smouldered deep in the heart of the baffled tyrant".

Then, as already noted, the atmosphere and incidents of *Eric* fail to carry conviction. Making every allowance for the eccentricities of people who lived sixty years ago, the modern boy simply refuses to credit the idea of members of a "decent" school indulging in "a superior titter" when one of their number performed the everyday feat of breaking down in translation. He finds it hard to believe that Owen (who is labelled with damning enthusiasm "a boy of mental superiority") would really report another boy for kicking him, and, quite incredible that after the kicker had been flogged the virtuous Owen should "have the keen mortification of seeing 'Owen is a sneak' written up all about the walls". As for Eric and Russell, sitting on a green bank beside the sea and "looking into one another's eyes and silently promising that they will be loving friends for ever" – the spectacle makes the undemonstrative young Briton physically unwell. Again, no schoolboy ever called lighted candles "superfluous abundance of nocturnal illumination"; and no schoolmaster under any circumstances ever "laid a gentle hand" upon a schoolboy's head. A hand, possibly, but not a gentle one. Lower School boys are not given Æschylus to read; and if they were they would not waste their play-hours discussing the best rendering of a particularly knotty passage occurring in a lesson happily over and done with.

If the first half of *Eric* is overdrawn and improbable, the second is rank melodrama – and bad melodrama at that. The trial scene is impossibly theatrical, and Russell's illness and death-bed deliverances are an outrage on schoolboy reserve.

Listen again to one Montagu, a sixth-form boy who has caught a gang of dormitory roysterers preparing an apple-pie bed for him. Does he call them "cheeky young swine", and knock their heads together? No!

> "'By heavens, this is *too* bad!' he exclaimed, stamping his foot with anger. 'What have I ever done to you young blackguards that you should treat me thus? Have I ever been a bully? Have I ever harmed one of you? And *you*, too, Vernon Williams!'
>
> "The little boy trembled and looked ashamed under his glance of sorrow and scorn.
>
> "'Well, I *know* who has put you up to this; but you shall not escape so. I shall thrash you, every one.'
>
> "Very quietly he suited the action to the word, sparing none."

These silent, strong men!

Again, do, or did, English schoolboys ever behave like this?

> "Vernon hid his face on Eric's shoulder; and, as his brother stooped over him and folded him to his heart, they cried in silence, for there seemed no more to say, until, wearied with sorrow, the younger fell asleep; and then Eric carried him tenderly downstairs, and laid him, still half-sleeping, upon his bed."

The characters in *Eric* are far superior to the incidents. They may be exaggerated and irritating, but they are consistently drawn. Wildney is a true type, and still exists. Russell is a fair specimen of a "good" boy, though it is difficult to feel for him the tenderness which most of us extend, perhaps furtively, to Arthur in *Tom Brown*. But some of the masters are beyond comprehension. Pious but depressing pedagogues of the type Mr. Rose (who at moments of crisis, it will be remembered, was usually to be found upon his knees in the School Library, oblivious of the greater privacy and comfort offered by his bedroom) have faded from our midst. Their place today is occupied by efficient and unsentimental young men in fancy waistcoats.

But the book for clear types is *Tom Brown*. East, the two Brookes, and Arthur – we recognise them all. There is Flashman the bully – an epitome of all bullies. He is of an everlasting pattern. And there is that curiously attractive person Martin, the scientist, with his jackdaw and his chemical research, and his chronic impecuniosity. You remember how he used to barter his allowance of candles for birds' eggs; with the result that, in those pre-gas-and-electricity days, he was reduced to doing his preparation by the glow of the fire, or "by the light of a flaring cotton wick, issuing from a ginger-beer bottle full of some doleful composition"? Lastly, there is Arnold himself. He is only revealed to us in glimpses: he emerges now and then like a mountain-peak from clouds; but is none the less imposing for that.

What impression of bygone schoolboy life do *Tom Brown* and *Eric* make upon our minds?

The outstanding sensation appears to be this, that fifty years ago life at school was more spacious than now – more full of incident and variety. In those days a boy's spare time was his own. How did he spend his half-holidays? If he was a good boy – good in the bad sense of the word – he went and sat upon a hill-top and admired the scenery, or thought of his mother, or possibly gripped another good boy by the hand and said: "Let me call you Edwin and you shall always call me Eric". If he was a normal healthy boy he went swimming, or bird-nesting, or (more usually) poaching, and generally encountered adventure by the way. If he was a bad boy he retired with other malefactors to a public-house, where he indulged in an orgy of roast goose and brandy-and-water.

Nous avons changé tout cela. Compulsory games have put an end to such licence, and in so doing have docked a good deal of liberty as well. The result has been to emphasize the type at the expense of the individual. It is a good type – a grand type – but it bears hardly upon some of its more angular components. The new system keeps the weak boy out of temptation and the idle boy out of mischief; but the quiet, reflective, unathletic boy hates it. He has little chance now to dream dreams or commune with nature. Still, his chance comes later in life; and as we all have to learn to toe the line at some time or another, thrice blessed is he who gets over the lesson in early youth.

The prefectorial system, too, has enlarged boys' sense of responsibility, and has put an end to many abuses which no master could ever reach. But on the whole we may say of the public-school boy throughout the ages that *plus que l'on le change, plus c'est la même chose*. Schoolboy gods have not altered. Strength, fleetness of foot, physical beauty, loyalty to one's House and one's School – youth still worships these things. There is the same admiration for *natural* brilliancy, be it in athletics or conversation or scholarship, and the same curious contempt for the plodder – even the successful plodder – in all departments of life. The weakest still goes to the wall. He is not bumped against it so vigorously as he used to be; but he still goes there, and always will.

Still, has the present generation developed no new characteristics? Let us turn to a batch of modern school stories, and see.

We have many to choose from – *Stalky*, for instance. *Stalky* has come in for a shower of abuse from certain quarters. He hits the sentimentalist hard. We are told that the book is vulgar, that the famous trio are "little beasts". (I think Mr. A. C. Benson said so.) Still, Mr. Kipling never touches any subject which he does not adorn, and in *Stalky* he brings out vividly some of the salient features of modern school life. He has drawn masters as they have never been drawn before: the portraits may be cruel, biased, not sufficiently representative; but how they live! He has put the case for the unathletic boy with convincing truth. He depicts, too, very faithfully, the curious *camaraderie* which prevails nowadays between boys and masters, and pokes mordant fun at the sycophancy which this state of things breeds in a certain type of boy – the "Oh, sir! and No, sir! and Yes, sir! and Please, sir!" brigade – and deals faithfully with the master who takes advantage of out-of-school intimacy to be familiar and offensive in school, addressing boys by their nicknames and making humorous reference to extra-scholastic incidents. And above all Mr. Kipling knows the heart of a boy. He understands, above all men, a boy's intense reserve upon matters that lie deepest within him, and his shrinking from and repugnance to unrestrained and blatant discussion of these things. Do you remember the story of the fat man – "the jelly-bellied flag-flapper" – who came down to lecture to the school on patriotism?

> "Now the reserve of a boy is tenfold deeper than the reserve of a maid, she having been made for one end only by blind Nature, but man for several. With a large and healthy hand he tore down these veils, and trampled them under the well-intentioned feel of eloquence. In a raucous voice he cried aloud little matters, like the hope of Honour and the dream of Glory, that boys do not discuss with their most intimate equals... He profaned the most secret places of their souls with outcries and gesticulations. He bade them consider the deeds of their ancestors, in such fashion that they were flushed to their tingling ears. Some of them – the rending voice cut a frozen stillness – might have had relatives who perished in defence of their country. (They thought, not a few of them, of an old sword in a passage, or above a breakfast-table, seen and fingered by stealth since they could walk.) He adjured them to emulate those illustrious examples; and they looked all ways in their extreme discomfort.
>
> "Their years forbade them even to shape their thoughts clearly to themselves. They felt savagely that they were being outraged by a fat man who considered marbles a game... What, in the name of everything caddish, was he driving at, who waved this horror before their eyes?"

It was a Union Jack, you will remember, suddenly unfurled by way or peroration.

"Happy thought! Perhaps he was drunk."

That is true, true, all through.

Then comes another class of school-story – the school-story written primarily *for* boys. Such are the books of Mr. Talbot Baines Reed. These are regarded as somewhat *vieux jeu* at the present day, but in their own particular line they have never been bettered. They were written to be read by comparatively young boys in a semi-religious magazine; and anybody who has ever attempted to write a tale which shall be probable yet interesting, and racy yet moral, will realise how admirably Mr. Reed has achieved this feat – in such books as *The Willoughby Captains*, *The Master of the Shell* and *The Fifth Form at St Dominic's*.

Another excellent book is *Godfrey Marten, Schoolboy*. Here Mr. Charles Turley achieves success by the most commendable means. He eschews the theatrical. His story contains no death-bed heroics; no rescues from drowning; no highly-coloured moral crises. He takes as his theme the humdrum daily life – and no one who has not lived through it for weeks at a time knows how humdrum it can be – of a public school, and makes it interesting. He lacks fire, it may be said, but he avoids the sentimentality of the old school and the cynicism of the new.

Perhaps the best of all this class is *The Bending of a Twig*, by Mr. Desmond Coke – an absolutely faithful picture, drawn with unerring instinct and refreshing humour. In fact it is so much the real thing that at times it is a trifle monotonous, just because school life at times is a trifle monotonous. But those who know what schoolboys are cannot fail to appreciate the intrinsic merits of this book. It gently derides the stagey incidents and emotional heroics of the old style of school story. Here a small boy comes to Shrewsbury primed with the lore of *Eric* and *Tom Brown* and *The Hill*, fully expecting to be tossed in a blanket or roasted on sight. But nothing happens: he is merely ignored. He has laboriously committed to memory a quantity of Harrow slang from *The Hill*: he finds this is meaningless at Shrewsbury. He cannot understand the situation: he has to unlearn all his lessons in sophistication. The whole thing is admirably done.

The story strikes a deeper note towards the end. Here we are given a very vivid study of the same boy, now head of his House, struggling between his sense of duty and the fear of unpopularity. Shall he tackle the disturbing element boldly, invoking if necessary the assistance of the Housemaster, or let things slide for the sake of peace? Many a tragedy of the Prefect's Room has hinged upon that struggle; and although Mr.

Coke's solution of the problem is not heroic, it is probably all the more true to life. Altogether a fine book, but from its very nature a book for boys rather than grown-ups.

Coming to the type of school-story at present in vogue, we have *The Hill*, deservedly ranking as first-class. But *The Hill* is essentially a book for Harrovians; and the more likely a book is to appeal to members of one particular school, the less likely it is to appeal to members of any other school. (In this respect we may note that *Tom Brown* forms an exception. But then *Tom Brown* is an exceptional book.) If *The Hill* had been written as a "general" school story, with the identity of Harrow veiled, however thinly, under a fictitious name, its glamour and romance, together with its enthusiasm for all that is straight and strong and of old standing and of good report, would have made it a classic among school fiction. But non-Harrovians – and there are a considerable number of them – decline with natural insularity to follow Mr. Vachell to his topmost heights. They are conscious of a clannish, slightly patronising air about *The Hill* which is notably absent in other stories which tell the tale of a particular school. The reader is treated to pedantic little footnotes, and given a good deal of information which is either gratuitous or uninteresting. He is made to understand that he is on The Hill but not of it. He recognises frankly enough the greatness of Harrow tradition and the glory of Harrow history, but he rightly reserves his enthusiasm over such things for his own school; and there are moments when he feels inclined to bawl out to the author that he envies Harrow nothing – except perhaps *Forty Years On*.

In other words, *The Hill*, owing to the insistent fashion in which it puts Harrow first and general schoolboy nature second, must be regarded more as a glorified prospectus than as a representative novel of English school life.

But *The Hill* stands high. It cannot be hid.

It is supersentimental at times, but then so are schoolboys. And the characters are clean-cut and finely finished. Scaife is a memorable figure; so is Warde. John Verney, like most virtuous persons, is a bit of a bore at times; but the Caterpillar, with his drawling little epigrams, and their inevitable tag – "Not my own; my Governor's!" – is a joy for ever. Lastly, the description of the Eton and Harrow Match at Lord's takes unquestionable rank as one of the few things in this world which will never be better done.

Two other books may be mentioned here, as illustrating the tendency, already mentioned, of modern school-novelists to shift the limelight from the boy to the master. The first is Mr. Hugh Walpole's *Mr. Perrin and Mr. Traill*. A young man lacking means, and possessing only a moderate degree, who feels inclined, as many do, to drift into schoolmastering as a *pis aller*, should read, mark, learn and inwardly digest this book. It draws a pitiless picture of Common Room life in a third-rate public school – the monotony; the discomfort; the mutual antagonism and jealousy of a body of men herded together year after year, condemned to celibacy by want of means, and deprived of all prospect of advancement or change of scene. It hammers in the undeniable truth that in the great majority of cases a schoolmaster's market value depreciates steadily from the date of his first appointment. *Mr. Perrin and Mr. Traill* is a very able book, but should not be read by schoolmasters while recovering, let us say, from influenza.

If the reader desires a further picture of the amenities of the Common Room, viewed from a less oblique angle, he can confidently be recommended to turn to *The Lanchester Tradition*, by Mr. G. F. Bradby. *The Lanchester Tradition* is a comparatively short story, but it is all pure gold. It is written with knowledge, insight, and above all with an appreciation of that broad tolerant humorous outlook on life which alone can lubricate the soul-grinding wheels of routine. In *Mr. Perrin and Mr. Traill* we have a young, able, and merciless critic exposing some of the weaknesses of the public-school system. In *The Lanchester Tradition* we have a seasoned and experienced representative of that system demonstrating that real character can always rise superior to circumstance, and that for all its creaking machinery and accompanying friction the pedagogue's existence can be a very tolerable and at times a very uplifting one. It is the old struggle between theory and practice. *Solvitur ambulando*.

There are many other school stories of recent date, of which no mention has been made in this survey; but our excursions seem to have covered a fairly representative field. What is the prevailing characteristic of the new, as compared with the old? It appears to be a very insistent and rather discordant note of realism – the sort of realism which leaves nothing unphotographed. Romance and sentiment are swept aside: they might fog the negative. Our rising generation are not permitted to see visions or dream dreams. And there is a tendency – mercifully absent in most of the books which we have described – to discuss matters which are better not discussed, at any rate in a work of fiction. There is a great vogue in these introspective days for outspokenness upon intimate matters. We are told that such matter should not be excluded from the text, because it is "true to life". So are the police reports in the Sunday newspapers; but we do not present files of these delectable journals to our sons and daughters – let us not forget the daughters: the sons go to school, but the daughters can only sit at home and read schoolboy stories – as Christmas presents.

There is another marked characteristic of modern school fiction – its intense topicality. The slang, the allusions, the incidents – they are all *dernier cri*. But the more up-to-date a thing may be, whether it be a popular catch-phrase or a whole book, the more ephemeral is its existence. A book of this kind reproduces the spirit of the moment, often with surprising fidelity; but after all it is only the spirit of the moment. Its very applicability to the moment unfits it for any other position. Books, speeches, and jokes – very few of these breathe the spirit not only of the moment but of all time. When they do, we call them Classics. *Tom Brown* is a Classic, and probably *Stalky* too. They are built of material which is imperishable, because it is quarried from the bed-rock of human nature, which never varies, though architectural fashions come and go.

Chapter Seven

"MY PEOPLE"

I

UNDER THIS comprehensive title the schoolboy groups the whole of his relatives, of both sexes.

"Are your people coming for Speech Day?" inquires Master Smith of Master Brown.

"Yes, worse luck!"

"It is a bore," agrees Smith. "I wanted you to come and sit with me."

"Sorry!" says Brown, and the matter ends.

It never occurs to Brown to invite Smith to join the family party. Such a proceeding would be unheard of. A schoolboy with his "people" in tow neither expects nor desires the society of his friends. His father may be genial, his mother charming, his sister pretty; but in the jaundiced eyes of their youthful host they are nothing more or less than a gang of lepers – to be segregated from all communication with the outer world; to be conveyed from one point to another as stealthily as possible; and above all to be kept out of the way of masters.

Later in life, say at the University, this diffidence disappears. A pretty sister becomes an asset; a pearl of price; a bait for luncheon parties and a trap for theatre-tickets. Even a father, provided he does not wear a made-up tie or take off his hat to the Dons, is tolerated. But at school – never! Why?

The reason is that it is almost impossible to give one's "people" their heads when on a visit to School without opening the way for breaches of etiquette and social outrages of the most deplorable kind. Left to themselves, fathers are addicted to entering into conversation with casual masters – especially masters who in the eyes of a boy are too magnificent to be approached or too despicable to be noticed. Mothers have been known to make unsolicited overtures to some School potentate – yea, even the Captain of the Eleven – because he happens to have curly hair or be wearing a pretty blazer. Sisters are capable of extending what the Lower School terms "the R.S.V.P. eye" to the meanest and most insignificant fag. These solecisms shame Master Brown to his very soul. Consequently he keeps his relatives in relentlessly close order, herding them across the quadrangle under a running fire of admonition and reproof.

"Yes, Dad, that's the Head. Look the other way, or he'll notice you ... For goodness sake, Mum, don't stop and talk to *this* fellow: he's in the Boat. *Who is that dear little boy with brown eyes?* Great Scott, how should I know all the rotten little ticks in the Lower School? ... Sis, what on earth did you go smiling and grinning at that chap for? He's a master. *He took his hat off?* Well, you must have begun it, that's all! Think what an outsider he must consider you! ... *What, Mum? Who are these two nice-looking boys sitting on that bench?* Not so loud! They're the Captain of the Eleven and the Secretary. *Will I ask them to tea to amuse Dolly?* Certainly, if you don't mind my leaving the School for good tomorrow morning! ... This is the cricket-ground. No, you can't go and sit in the shade under those trees: it is fearful side to go there. Stay about here. If you see any people you know, from Town or anywhere, you can talk to them; but whatever you do, don't go making up to chaps. I'll find young Griffin for you if you like. He'll be pretty sick; but he knows you in the holidays, so I suppose he has got to go through it. Sit here. Perhaps you had better not speak to *anybody* while I'm away, whether you know them or not. Sis, remember about not making eyes at fellows. They don't like that sort of thing from young girls: they're different from your pals in Hyde Park; so hold yourself in. I'll be back in a minute."

Then he departs in search of the reluctant Griffin.

The only member of the staff to whom a boy permits his "people" to address themselves is his Housemaster. Him he regards as inevitable; and consents gloomily to conduct his tainted band to a ceremonial tea in the Housemaster's drawing-room. There he sits miserably upon the edge of a chair, masticating cake, and hoping against hope that the ceremony will end before his relatives have said or done something particularly disastrous.

He is conscious, too, of a sad falling-off in his own demeanour. Ten minutes ago he was a miniature Grand Turk, patronising his parents and ruffling it over his sister. Now he is a rather grubby little hobbledehoy, conscious of large feet and red hands, mumbling "Yes, sir" and "No, sir" to a man whom he has been accustomed to represent to his family as being wax in his hands and a worm in his presence.

An observant philosopher once pointed out that in every man there are embedded three men: first, the man as he appears to himself; second, the man as he appears to others; third, the man as he really is. This classification of points of view is particularly applicable to the scholastic world. Listen, for instance, to Master Smith, describing to an admiring circle of sisters and young brothers a scene from school life as it is lived in the Junior Remove.

"*Is the work difficult?* Bless you, we don't do any work: we just rot Duck-face. We simply rag his soul out. *What do we do to him?* Oh, all sorts of things. *What sort?* Well, the other day he started up his usual song about the necessity of absolute attention and concentration – great word of Duck-face's, concentration – and gave me an impot for not keeping my eyes fixed on him all the time he was jawing. I explained to him that anybody who attempted such a feat would drop down dead in five minutes. *How dare I say such a thing to a master?* Well, I didn't say it in so many words, but he knew what I meant all right. He got pretty red. After that I tipped the wink to the other chaps, and we all stared at him till he simply sweated. Oh, we give him a rotten time!"

Mr. Duckworth's version of the incident, in the Common Room, ran something like this.

"What's that, Allnutt? *How is young Smith getting on?* Let me see – Smith? Oh, that youth! I remember him now. Well, he strikes me as being not far removed from the idiot type, but he is perfectly harmless. I don't expect ever to teach him anything, of course, but he gives no trouble. He is quite incapable of concentrating his thoughts on anything for more than five minutes without constant ginger from me. I had to drop rather heavily upon him this morning, and the results were most satisfactory. He was attentive for quite half an hour. But he's a dull customer."

What really happened was this. Mr. Duckworth, who was a moderate disciplinarian and an extremely uninspiring teacher, had occasion to set Master Smith fifty lines for inattention. Master Smith, glaring resentfully and muttering muffled imprecations – symptoms of displeasure which Mr. Duckworth, who was a man of peace at any price, studiously ignored – remained comparatively attentive for the rest of the hour and ultimately showed up the lines.

All this time we have left our young friend Master Brown sitting upon the edge of a chair in his Housemaster's drawing-room, glaring defiantly at everyone and wondering what awful thing his "people" are saying now.

Occasionally scraps of conversation reach his ears. (He is sitting over by the window with his sister.) His mother is doing most of the talking. The heads of her discourse appear in the main to be two – the proper texture of her son's undergarments, and the state of his soul. The Housemaster, when he gets a chance, replies soothingly. The Matron shall be instructed to see that nothing is discarded prematurely during the treacherous early summer: he himself will take steps to have Reggie – the boy blushing hotly at the sound of his Christian name on alien lips – prepared for confirmation with the next batch of candidates.

Occasionally his father joins in.

"I expect we can safely leave that question to Mr. Allnutt's discretion, Mary," he observes drily. "After all, Reggie is not the only boy in the House."

"No, I am sure he is not," concedes Mrs. Brown. "But I know you won't object to hear the *mother's* point of view, will you, Mr. Allnut?"

"I fancy Mr. Allnutt has heard the mother's point of view once or twice before," interpolates Mr. Brown, with a sympathetic smile in the direction of the Housemaster.

"Now, John," says Mrs. Brown playfully, "don't interfere! Mr. Allnutt and I understand one another perfectly, don't we, Mr. Allnutt?"

She takes up her parable again with renewed zest. "You see, Mr.

Allnutt, what I mean is, you are a bachelor. You have never had any young people to bring up, so naturally you can't *quite* appreciate, as I can–"

Mr. Allnutt, who has brought up about fifty "young people" per annum for fifteen years, smiles wanly, and bows to the storm. Master Brown, almost at the limit of human endurance, glances despairingly at his sister. That tactful young person grasps the situation, and endeavours to divert the conversation.

"What pretty cups those are on that shelf," she says in a clear voice to her brother. "Are they Mr. Allnutt's prizes?"

"Yes," replies Master Brown, with a sidelong glance towards his Housemaster. But that much-enduring man takes no notice: his attention is still fully occupied by Mrs. Brown, whom he now darkly suspects of having a suitable bride for him concealed somewhere in her peroration.

Master Brown and his sister rise to inspect the collection of trophies more closely.

"What a lot he has got," says Miss Brown, in an undertone now. "Was he a great athlete?"

"He thinks he was. When he gets in a bait over anything it is always a sound plan to get him to talk about one of these rotten things. I once got off a tanning by asking him how many times he had been Head of the River. As a matter of fact, most of these are prizes for chess, or tricycling, or something like that."

So the joyous libel proceeds. Master Reggie is beginning to cheer up a little.

"What is that silver bowl for?" inquires his sister.

"Ah, it takes him about half an hour to tell you about that. They won the race by two feet in record time, and he was in a dead faint for a week afterwards. As a matter of fact, Bailey tertius, whose governor was up at Oxford with the old Filbert" – etymologists will have no difficulty in tracing this synonym to its source – "says that he saw the race, and that Filbert caught a crab and lost his oar about five yards from the start and was a passenger all the way. The men on the bank yelled to him to jump out, but he was in too big a funk of being drowned, and wouldn't. Of course he doesn't know we know!" And so the joyous libel proceeds.

And yet, in Reggie Brown's last half-term report we find the words: *A conscientious, but somewhat stolid and unimaginative boy.*

II

But "people" do not visit the School solely for the purpose of bringing social disaster upon their offspring. Their first visit, at any rate, is of a very different nature. On this occasion they come in the capacity of what Headmasters call "prospective parents" – that is, parents who propose to inspect the School with a view to entering a boy – and as such are treated with the deference due to imperfectly hooked fish.

The prospective parent varies considerably. Sometime he is an old member of the School, and his visit is a purely perfunctory matter. He knows every inch of the place. He lunches with the Head, has a talk about old times, and mentions with proper pride that yet another of his boys is now of an age to take up his nomination for his father's old House.

Then comes another type – the youthful parent. Usually he brings his wife with him. He is barely forty, and has not been near a school since he left his own twenty years ago. His wife is pretty, and not thirty-five. Both feel horribly juvenile in the presence of the Head. They listen deferentially to the great man's pontifical observations upon the requirements of modern education, and answer his queries as to their firstborn's age and attainments with trembling exactitude.

"I think we shall be able to lick him into shape," concludes the Head, with gracious jocularity. It is mere child's play to him, handling parents of this type.

Then the male bird plucks up courage, and timidly asks a leading question. The Head smiles.

"Ah!" he remarks. "Now you are laying an invidious task upon me. Who am I, to discriminate between my colleagues' Houses?"

The young parents apologise precipitately, but the Head says there is no need. In fact, he goes so far as to recommend a House – in strict confidence.

"Between ourselves," he says, "I consider that *the* man here at the present moment is Mr. Rotterson. Send your boy to him. I *believe* he has a vacancy for next term, but you had better see him at once. I will give you a note for him now. There you are! Good morning!"

Off hurry the anxious pair. But the telephone outstrips them.

"Is that you, Rotterson?" says the Head. "I have just despatched a brace of parents to you. Impress them! There are prospects of more tomorrow, so with any luck we ought to be able to pull up your numbers to a decent level after all."

"Thank you very much," says a meek voice at the other end.

Then there is the bluff, hearty parent – the man who knows exactly what he wants, and does not hesitate to say so.

"I don't want my son taught any of your new-fangled nonsense," he explains breezily. "Just a good sound education, without frills! The boy will have to earn his own living afterwards, and I want you to teach him something which will enable him to do so. Don't go filling him up with Latin and Greek: give him something which will be useful in an office. I know you pedagogues stick obstinately to what you call a good general grounding; but, if I may say so, you ought to *specialise* a bit more. You're too shy of specialisation, you know. But I say: Find out what each boy in your School requires for his future career, and teach him *that!*"

A Headmaster once replied to a parent of this description:

"Unfortunately, sir, the fees of this school and the numbers of its Staff are calculated upon a *table d'hôte* basis. If you want to have your son educated *à la carte*, you must get a private tutor for him."

Then there is the Utterly Impossible parent. He is utterly impossible for one of two reasons – either because he is a born faddist, or because he has relieved Providence of a grave responsibility by labelling himself "A Self-Made Man, and Proud of It!"

The faddist is the sort of person who absorbs Blue Books without digesting them, and sits upon every available Board without growing any wiser, and cherishes theories of his own about non-competitive examinations, and cellular underclothing, and the use of graphs and, generally speaking, about every subject on which there is no particular reason why the layman should hold any opinions at all. Such a creature harries the scholastic profession into premature senility. Him the Head always handles in the same fashion. He delivers him over at the first opportunity to a Housemaster, and the Housemaster promptly takes him out on to the cricket-field and, having introduced him to the greatest bore upon the Staff, leaves the pair together to suffer the fate of the Kilkenny cats.

The other sort of Utterly Impossible is not so easily scotched. The ordinary snubs of polite society are not for him. He is a plain man, he mentions, and likes to put things on a business footing. Putting things on a business footing seems to necessitate – no one knows why – a recital of the plain man's early struggles, together with a *resumé* of his present bank-balance and directorships. Not infrequently he brings his son with him, and having deposited that shrinking youth on a chair under the eyes both of the Head and himself, proceeds to run over his points with enormous gusto and unparental impartiality.

"There he is!" he bellow. "Now you've *got* him! Ram it into him! Learn him to be a scholar, and I'll pay any bill you like to send in. I've got the dibs. He's not a bad lad, as lads go, but he wants his jacket dusted now and then. My father dusted mine regular every Saturday night for fifteen year, and it made me the man I am. I'm worth–"

A condensed Budget follows. Then the harangue is resumed.

"So don't spare the rod – that's what I say. Learn him all that a scholar ought to be learned. If he wants books, get them, and put them down to me. I can pay for them. And at the end of the year, if he gets plucked in his examinations, you send him home to me, and I'll bile him!"

The plain man breaks off, and glares with ferocious affection upon his offspring. All this while the shrewd Head has been observing the boy's demeanour; and if he decides that the exuberance of his papa has not been inherited to an ineradicable extent, he accepts the cowering youth and does his best for him. As a rule he is justified in his judgment.

Lastly comes a novel and quite inexplicable variant of the species. It owes its existence entirely to journalistic enterprise.

Little Tommy Snooks, we will say, arrives home one afternoon in a taxi in the middle of term, and announces briefly but apprehensively to his parents that he has been "sacked". He is accompanied or preceded by a letter from his Headmaster, expressing genuine sorrow for the occurrence, and adding that though it has been found necessary for the sake of discipline to remove Master Thomas from the School, his offence has not been such as to involve any moral stigma. Little Tommy's parents, justly incensed that their offspring should have been expelled from school without incurring any moral stigma, write demanding instant reparation. The Headmaster, in his reply, states that Thomas has been expelled because he has broken a certain rule, the penalty for breaking which happens to be – and is known to be – expulsion. *Voilà tout.* In other words, he has been expelled, not for smoking or drinking or breaking bounds (or whatever he may happen to have done), but for deliberately and wantonly flying in the face of the Law which prohibits these misdemeanours. Either Tommy must go, or the Law be rendered futile and ridiculous.

This paltry and frivolous attempt to evade the real point at issue – which appears to be that many people, including Tommy's parents and the Headmaster himself, smoke, drink, and go out after dark and are none the worse – is treated with the severity which it deserves. A letter is despatched, consigning the Headmaster to scholastic perdition. The Headmaster briefly acknowledges receipt, and suggests that the correspondence should now cease.

So far the campaign has followed well-defined and perfectly natural lines, for a parent is seldom disposed to take his boy's expulsion "lying down". But at this point the new-style parent breaks right away from tradition – kicks over the traces, in fact. Despatching that slightly dazed but on the whole deeply gratified infant martyr, Master Tommy, to salve outraged nature at an adjacent Picture Palace, the parent sits down at his (or her) desk and unmasks the whole dastardly conspiracy to a halfpenny newspaper of wide circulation. "I do this," he explains, "not from any feeling of animosity towards the Headmaster of the School, but in order to clear my son's good name and fair fame in the eyes of the world." This is interesting and valuable news to the world, which has not previously heard of Tommy Snooks. The astute editor of the halfpenny paper, with a paternal smile upon his features and his tongue in his cheek, publishes the letter in a conspicuous position – if things in the football and political world happen to be particularly dull, he sometimes finds room for Tommy's photograph too – and invites general correspondence on the subject.

Few parents can resist such an opportunity; and for several weeks the editor is supplied, free gratis, with a column of diversified but eminently saleable matter. The beauty of a controversy of this kind is that you can debate upon almost any subject without being pulled up for irrelevance. Parents take full advantage of this licence. Some contribute interesting legends of their children's infancy. Others plunge into a debate upon punishment in general, and the old battle of cane, birch, slipper, imposition, detention, and moral suasion is fought over again. This leads to a discussion as to whether public schools shall or shall not be abolished – by whom, is not stated. Presently the national reserve of retired colonels is mobilised, and fiery old gentlemen write form Cheltenham to say that in their young days boys were boys and not molly-coddles. Old friends like *Materfamilias*, *Pro Bono Publico*, *Quis Custodiet Custodes* rush into the fray with joyous whoops. There is quite a riot of pseudonyms: the only person who gives his proper name (and address) is the headmaster of a small preparatory school, who contributes a copy of his prospectus, skilfully disguised as a treatise on "How to Preserve Home Influences at School".

But the boom is short-lived. Presently a crisis arises in some other department of our national life. Something cataclysmal happens to the House of Commons, or the Hippodrome, or Tottenham Hotspur. Public attention is diverted; the correspondence is closed with cruel abruptness; and little Tommy Snooks is summoned from the Picture Palace, and sent to another school or provided with a private tutor. Still, his good name and fair fame are now vindicated in the eyes of the world.

But it is not altogether surprising that the great Temple should once have observed: "Boys are always reasonable; masters sometimes; parents, never!"

III

Correspondence between school and home is conducted upon certain well-defined lines. A boy writes home every Sunday: his family may write to him when they please and as often as they please. But – they must never send postcards.

Postcards in public schools are common property. Many a new boy's promising young life has been overclouded at the very outset by the arrival of some such maternal indiscretion as this:

Dearest Artie,

    I am sending you some nice new vests for the colder months. Mind you put them on, but ask the Matron to air them first. The girls send their love, and Baby sends you a kiss.

Yours affec.
Mother.

"Dearest Artie" usually comes into possession of this missive after it has been passed from hand to hand, with many joyous comments, the whole length of the Lower School breakfast table. He may not hear the last of the vests and Baby for months.

As for writing home, a certain elasticity of method is essential. In addressing one's father, it is advisable to confine oneself chiefly to the topic of one's studies. Money should not be asked for, but references to the Classics may be introduced with advantage, and perhaps a fair copy of one's last Latin prose enclosed. The father will not be able to understand or even read it; but this will not prevent him from imagining that he could have done so thirty years ago; and his heart will glow with the reminiscent enthusiasm of the retired scholar.

Mothers may be addressed with more freedom. Small financial worries may be communicated, and it is a good plan to dwell resignedly but steadily upon the insufficiency of the food supplied by the School authorities. Health topics may be discussed, especially in so far as they touch upon the question of extra diet.

Sisters appreciate School gossip and small talk of any kind.

Young brothers may be impressed with daredevil tales of masters put to rout and prefects "ragged" to death.

The appended *dossier* furnishes a fairly comprehensive specimen of the art. It is entitled:

THE BIRTHDAY

Correspondence addressed to Master E Bumpleigh,
Mr. Killick's House, Grandwich School

No. 1

MESSRS BUMPLEIGH & SITWELL LTD
220B CORNHILL
Telegrams: "BUMPSIT, LONDON"
November 6, 19—

MY DEAR EGBERT,

Your mother informs me that tomorrow, the 7th inst., is your fifteenth birthday. I therefore take this opportunity of combining my customary greetings with a few observations on your half-term report, which has just reached me. It is a most deplorable document. With the exception of your health (which is described as "excellent"), and your violin-playing (which I note is "most energetic), I can find no cause for congratulation or even satisfaction in your record for the past half-term. Indeed, were it not for the existence of the deep-seated conspiracy (of which you have so frequently and so earnestly warned me) among the masters at your school, to deprive you of your just marks and so prevent you from taking your rightful place at the head of the form, I should almost suspect you of idling.

I enclose ten shillings as a birthday gift. If you could contrive during the next half-term to overcome the unfortunate prejudice with which the Grandwich staff appears to be inspired

"My People"

against you, I might see my way to doing something rather more handsome at Christmas. –

Your affectionate father
JOHN HENRY BUMPLEIGH.

(*Reply.*

November 7

MY DEAR FATHER,

Thanks awfully for the ten bob. Yes, it is most deplorable as you say about my report. I feel it very much. It is a rum thing that I should have come out bottom, for I have been working fearfully hard lately. I expect a mistake has been made in adding up the marks. You see, they are sent in to the form-master at half-term, and he, being a classical man, naturally can't do mathematics a bit, so he adds up the marks all anyhow, and practically anybody comes out top. It is very dishartening. I think it would better if I went on the Modern Side next term. The masters there are just as ignerant and unfair as on the classical, but not being classical men they do know something about adding up marks. So if I went I might get justice done me. I must now stop, as I have several hours more prep. to do, and I want to go and ask Mr. Killick for leave to work on after bed-time.

Your affec. Son,
E. BUMPLEIGH.

No. 2

THE LIMES, WALLOW-IN-THE WEALD, SURREY, *Monday*

MY DEAREST BOY,

Very many happy returns for your birthday. The others (*Genealogical Tree omitted here*) ... send their best love.

I fear your father is not quite pleased with your half-term

report. It seems a pity you cannot get higher up in your form, but I am sure you *try*, my boy. I don't think Father makes quite enough allowance for your health. With your weak digestion, long hours of sedentary work must be very trying at times. Ask the matron ... (*one page omitted*). I enclose ten shillings, and will send you the almond cake and potted lobster you ask for.

Your affectionate mother,
MARTHA BUMPLEIGH.

(*Reply.*

November 7

DEAR MUM,

Thanks ever so much for the ten bob, also the lobster and cake, which are A1. Yes, the pater wrote to me about my report – rather a harsh letter, I thought. Still, we must make allowances for him. When he was young education was a very simple matter. Now it is the limit. My digestion is all right, thanks, but my head aches terribly towards the end of a long day of seven or eight hours' work. Don't mention this to the pater, as it might worry him. I shall work on to the end, but if the strain gets too much it might be a sound plan for me to go on the Modern Side next term. You might mention this cassualy to the pater. I must stop now, as the prayer-bell is ringing.

Your affect. Son,
E. BUMPLEIGH.)

No. 3

THE LIMES, WALLOW-IN-THE-WEALD, SURREY, *Aujourd' hui*

DEAR EGGIE,

Many happy returns. I have spent all my dress allowance, so I can't do much in the way of a present, I'm afraid; but I send a P.O. for *2s. 6d.* You got a pretty bad half-term report, my dear. Breakfast that morning was a cheery meal. I got hold of it afterwards and read it, and certainly you seem to have been getting into hot water all round. By the way, I see you have got some new masters at Grandwich, judging by the initials on your report. I know "V.K." and "O.P.H.": they are Killick and Higginson, aren't they? But who are "A.C.N." and "M.P.G."?

Your affect. Sister,
BARBARA.

(*Reply*.)

DEAR BABS,

Thanks ever so much for the *2s. 6d*. It is most welcome, as the pater only sent ten bob, being shirty about my report; and the mater another. Still, I haven't heard from Aunt Deborah yet: she usually comes down hansom on my birthday. The new masters you mean are A. C. Newton and M. P. Gainford. I don't think either of them would take very kindly to you. Newton is an International, so he won't have much use for girls. Gainford is rather a snipe, and has been married for years and years. But I'll tell you if any more new ones come. I am making a last effort to get on to the Mods. next term – about fed up with Higgie.

Your affect. Brother.
E. BUMPLEIGH.

No. 4

THE SCHOOL HOUSE, OAKSHOTT SCHOOL, BUCKS, *Monday*

DEAR EGGSTER,

Well, old sport, how goes it? Just remembered it is your birthday, so send you *9d*. in stamps – all I have but *2d*. How is your mangy school? Wait till our XV plays you on the 18th! What ho!

Your affec. brother.
J. BUMPLEIGH.

Just had a letter from the pater about my half-term report. He seems in a fairly rotten state.

(*Reply.*

November 7

DEAR MOPPY,

Thanks awfully for the *9d*. I am about broke, owing to my half-term report coninsiding with my birthday. Putrid luck, I call it. Still, Aunt Deborah hasn't weighed in yet. All right, send along your bandy-legged XV, and we will return them to you knock-kneed. I must stop now, as we are going to rag a man's study for wearing a dickey.

Your affect. brother,
E. BUMPLEIGH.)

No. 5

THE LABURNUMS, SURBITON, *Monday, Nov. 6*

MY DEAR NEPHEW,

Another year has gone by, and once more I am reminded that my little godson is growing up to a man's estate. Your fifteenth birthday! And I remember when you were only – (*Here Master Egbert skips three sheets and comes to the last page of the letter*) ... I am sending you a birthday present – something of greater value than usual. It is a handsome and costly edition of *Forty Years of Missionary Endeavour in Eastern Polynesia*, recently published. The author has actually signed his name upon the fly-leaf for you. Think of that! The illustrations are by an Associate of the Royal Academy. I hope you are well, and pursuing your studies diligently.

Your affectionate aunt,
DEBORAH SITWELL.

(*Reply.*

November 7

DEAR AUNT DEBORAH,

    Thank you very much for so kindly remembering my birthday. The book has just arrived, and I shall always look upon it as one of my most valuable possessions. I will read it constantly – whenever I have time, in fact; but really after being in school hard at work for ten or twelve hours a day, one is more inclined for bed than books, even one on such an absorbing subject as this. I am much interested in Missionary Endeavours, and help them in every way I can. We are having a sermon on the subject next Sunday. There is to be a collection, and I intend to make a special effort.

Your affect. nephew.
E. BUMPLEIGH.)

• • • •

Extract from the Catalogue of the Killickite House Library, Grandwich School:

"*Forty Years of Missionary Endeavour in Eastern Polynesia.* Presented by E. Bumpleigh, Nov. 8."

Chapter Eight

THE FATHER OF THE MAN

I

AMONG THE higher English castes it is not good form to appear deeply interested in anything, or to hold any serious views about anything, or to possess any special knowledge about anything. In fact, the more you know the less you say, and the more passionately you are interested in a matter, the less you "enthuse" about it. That is the Public School Attitude in a nutshell. It is a pose which entirely misleads foreigners and causes them to regard the English as an incredibly stupid and indifferent nation.

An American gentleman, we will say, with all an American's insatiable desire to "see the wheels go round" and get to the root of the matter, finds himself sitting beside a pleasant English stranger at a public dinner. They will converse, possibly about sport, or politics, or wireless telegraphy. The pleasant Englishman may be one of the best game shots in the country, or a Privy Councillor, or a scientist of European reputation, but the chances are that the American will never discover from the conversation that he is anything more than a rather superficial or diffident amateur. Again, supposing the identity of the stranger is known: the American will endeavour to draw him out. But the expert will decline to enter deeply into his own subject, for that would be talking "shop"; and under no circumstances will he consent to discuss his own achievements therein, for that would be "side".

Shop and Side – let us never lose sight of them. An Englishman dislikes brains almost as much as he worships force of character. If you call him "clever" he will regard you with resentment and suspicion. To his mind cleverness is associated with moral suppleness and sharp practice. In politics he may describe the leader of the other side as "clever"; but not his own leader. He is "able". But the things that he fears most are "shop" and "side". He is so frightened of being thought to take a pleasure in his work – he likes it to be understood that he only does it because he has to – and so terrified of being considered egotistical, that he prefers upon the whole to be regarded as lazy or dunderheaded. In most cases the brains are there, and the cleverness is there, and above all the passion for and pride in his work are there; but he prefers to keep these things to himself and present a careless or flippant front to the world.

From what does this national self-consciousness spring? It has its roots, as already indicated, in the English public school system.

Consider. The public school boy, like all primitive types, invents his own gods and worships them without assistance. Now the primitive mind recognises two kinds of god – lovable gods and gods which must be squared. Class A are worshipped from sheer admiration and reverence, because they are good and "able" gods, capable of godlike achievements. To Class B, however, homage is rendered as a pure measure of precaution, lest, being enormously powerful and remarkably uncertain in temper, they should turn and rend their votaries. Indeed, in their anxiety to avoid the unfavourable notice of these deities, the worshippers do not hesitate to sacrifice one another. So it is with the schoolboy. Class A consists of the gods he admires, Class B of the gods he is afraid of.

First, Class A.

What a boy admires most of all is ability – ability to do things, naturally and spontaneously. He worships bodily strength, bodily grace, swiftness of foot, straightness of eye, dashing courage and ability to handle a bat or gun, or control the movements of a ball, with dexterity and – ease. Great emphasis must be placed on the ease. Owing to a curious kink in the schoolboy mind, these qualities are not *natural* qualities – that is, if they have been acquired by laborious practice or infinite pains. The water-funk who ultimately schools himself into a brilliant high-diver, or the overgrown crock who trains himself, by taking thought, into an effective athlete, is a person of no standing. At school sports you often hear such a conversation as this:

"Good time for the mile, wasn't it?"

"Yes, but look at the way he has been sweating up for it. He's been in training for weeks. Did you see Jinks in the high jump, though? He cleared five foot four, and never turned out to practice once. That's pretty hot stuff if you like!"

Or:

"Pretty useful, old Dobbin taking six wickets!"

"Oh, that rotter! Last year he could hardly get the ball within a yard of the crease. I hear he has been spending hours and hours in the holidays bowling by himself at a single stump. He's no earthly good, really."

It is the way of the world. The tortoise is a dreadfully unpopular winner. To an Englishman, a real hero is a man who wins a championship in the morning, despite the fact that he was dead drunk the night before.

This contempt for the plodder extends also to the scholastic sphere. A boy has no great love or admiration for learning in itself, but he appreciates brilliance in scholarship – as opposed to hard work. If you come out top of your form, or gain an entrance scholarship at the University, your friends will applaud you vigorously, but only if they are perfectly certain that you have done no work whatever. If you are suspected of midnight oil or systematic labour, the virtue is gone out of your performance. You are merely a "swot". The general attitude appears to be that unless you can take – or appear to take – an obstacle in your stride, that obstacle is not worth surmounting. This leads to a good deal of hypocrisy and make-believe. For instance:

"Pretty good, Sparkleigh getting a Schol, wasn't it?" remark the rank and file to one another. "He never did a stroke of work for it, and when he went up for his exam, he went on the bust the night before. Jolly good score off the Head: he said he wouldn't get one! … Grubbe? Oh yes, he got one all right. I should just think so! The old sap! We'd have rooted him if he hadn't!"

But let us be quite frank about Sparkleigh. He has won his Scholarship, and has done it – in the eyes of the School – with one hand tied behind him. But Scholarships are not won in this way, and no one is better aware of the fact than Sparkleigh. His task, to tell the truth, has been far more difficult than that of the unheroic Grubbe. Grubbe was content to accept the stigma of "swot" because it carried with it permission to work as hard and as openly – one had almost said as flagrantly – as he pleased. But Sparkleigh, who had to maintain the attitude of a man of the world and a scholastic Gallio and yet work just as hard as Grubbe, was sorely put to it at times. He must work, and work desperately hard, yet never be seen working. None of his friends who slapped him on the back when the news of his success arrived knew of the desperate resorts to which the boy had had recourse in order to obtain the time and privacy necessary for his purpose. On Sunday afternoons he would disappear upon a country walk, ostentatiously exhibiting a cigarette cases and giving his friends to understand that his walk was the statutory three-mile qualification of a *bona-fide* traveller. In reality he sat behind a hedge in an east wind and contended with Thucydides.

And there was his demeanour in school. On Thursdays, for instance, the Sixth came in from four till six and composed Latin Verses. On these occasions the Head seldom appeared, the task of presiding over the drowsy assembly falling to a scholarly but timid young man who was mortally afraid of the magnates who sat at the top bench. Sparkleigh would take down the appointed passage as it was dictated and read it through carelessly. In reality he was committing it to memory. Then:

"Wake me at a quarter to six," he would say to his neighbour, yawning. And laying his head upon his arms, he would rest motionless until aroused at the appointed moment.

But he was not asleep. Four an hour and three-quarters that busy fertile brain would be pulling and twisting the English verse into Latin shape, converting it into polished Elegiacs or rolling hexameters. Then, sleepily raising his head, and casting a last contemptuous glance over the English copy, Sparkleigh would take up his pen, and in the remaining quarter of an hour scribble out a full and complete fair copy – to the respectful admiration of his neighbour Grubbe, who, covered with ink and surrounded by waste paper, was laboriously grappling with the last couplet.

There are many Sparkleighs in school life – and in the larger world as well. They are not really deceitful or pretentious, but they are members of a society in which revealed ambition is not good form. That is all.

There is one curious relaxation of the schoolboy's vendetta against ostentatious industry. You may work if you are a member of the Army Class. The idea appears to be that to cultivate learning for its own sake is the act of a pedant and a prig, but if you have some loyal, patriotic, and gentlemanly object in view such as the obtaining of the King's Commission, a little vulgar application of your nose to the grindstone may be excused and indeed justified. But you must be careful to explain that you are never, never going to do any work again after this.

As already noted, these characteristics puzzle the foreigner. The Scotsman, for instance, though even more reserved than the Englishman, is not nearly so self-conscious; and to him "ma career" – to quote John Shand – is the most important business in life. Success is far too momentous a thing to be jeopardised by false modesty; so why waste time and spoil one's chances by pretending that it is a mere accident in life – the gift of chance or circumstance? The American, too, cannot understand the pose. His motto is "Thorough". American oarsmen get their crew together a year before the race and train continuously – even in winter they row in a stationary tub under cover – until by diligent practice they evolve a perfect combination. Englishmen would never dream of taking such pains. They have a vague feeling that such action is "unsportsmanlike". In their eyes it is rather improper to appear so anxious to win. Once more we find ourselves up against the shame of revealed ambition. The public school spirit again!

So much for the gods a boy admires. Now for the gods he is afraid of.
The greatest of these is Convention. The first, and perhaps the only, thing that a boy learns at a public school is to keep in his appointed place. If he strays out by so much as a single pace, he is "putting on side", and is promptly sacrificed. Presumption is the deadliest sin in school life, and

is usually punished with a ferocity out of all proportion to the offence. In moderation, Convention is a very salutary deity. None of us are of much use in this world until we have found our level and acquired the virtues of modesty and self-suppression. It is extremely good for a cheeky new boy, late cock of a small preparatory school and idol of a doting family, to have to learn by painful experience that it is not for him to raise his voice in the course of general conversation or address himself to any but his own immediate order until he has been a member of the school for a year at least. These are what may be termed self-evident conventions, and it does no one any particular harm to learn to obey them. But the great god Convention, like most absolute monarchs, has grown distinctly cranky and eccentric in some of his whims. A sensible new boy knows better than to speak familiarly to a superior, or take a seat too near the fire, or answer back when unceremoniously treated. But there are certain laws of Convention which cannot be anticipated by the most intelligent and well-meaning beginner. For instance, it may be – and invariably is – "side" to wear your cap straight (or crooked), or your jacket buttoned (or unbuttoned), or your hair brushed (or not). But which? It is impossible to solve these problems by any process save that of dismal experience. And, as in a maturer branch of criminology, ignorance of the Law is held to be no excuse for infraction of the Law. I once knew a small boy who, trotting back to his House from football and being pressed for time, tied his new white sweater round his neck by the sleeves instead of donning it in the ordinary fashion. That evening, to his great surprise and extreme discomfort, he was taken out and slippered by a self-appointed vigilance committee. To wear one's sweater tied round one's neck, it seemed, was the privilege of the First Fifteen alone. Who shall tell how oft he offendeth?

And even when the first years are past and a position of comparative prominence attained, the danger of Presumption is not outdistanced. A boy obtains his House colours, we will say. His friends congratulate him warmly, and then sit down to wait for symptoms of "side". The newly-born celebrity must walk warily. Too often he trips. Our first success in life is very, very sweet, and it is hard to swallow our exultation and preserve a modest or unconscious demeanour when our heart is singing. But the lesson must be learned, and ultimately is learned; but too often only after a cruel and utterly disproportionate banishment to the wilderness. Can we wonder that the Englishman who has achieved greatness in the world – the statesman, the soldier, the athlete – always exhibits an artificial indifference of manner when his deeds are mentioned in his presence? In nine cases out of ten this is not due to proverbial heroic modesty: it is cased by painful and lasting memories of the results which followed his first essays in self-esteem.

The other god which schoolboys dread is Public Opinion. They have little fear of their masters, and none whatever of their parents; but they are mortally afraid of one another. Moral courage is the rarest thing in schoolboy life. Physical courage, on the other hand, is a *sine qua non*: so much so that if a boy does not possess it he must pretend he does. But if he exhibits moral courage the great majority of his fellows will fail to recognise it, and will certainly not appreciate it. They do not know its meaning. Their fathers have extolled it to them, and they have heard it warmly commended in sermons in chapel; but they seldom know it when they meet it. If an obscure and unathletic prefect reports a muscular and prominent member of the House to the Housemaster for some gross and demoralising offence, they will not regard the prefect as a hero. Probably they will consider him a prig, and certainly a sneak. The fact that he has sacrificed all that makes schoolboy life worth living in the exercise of his simple duty will not occur to the rank and file at all. Admiration for that sort of thing they regard as an idiosyncrasy of pastors and masters.

It is not until he becomes a prefect himself that the average boy discovers the meaning of the word character, and whether he possesses any of his own. If he does, he begins straightaway to make up for lost time. He sets yet another god upon his Olympus and keeps him at the very summit thereof from that day forth for the rest of his life. As already noted, the Englishman is suspicious of brains, despises intellectuality, and thoroughly mistrusts any superficial appearance of cleverness; but he worships character, character, character all the time. And that is the main – the only – difference between the English man and the English boy. The man appreciates moral courage, because it is a sign of character. It is the only respect in which the English Peter Pan grows up.

Finally, we note a new factor in the composition of the Public School Type – the military factor. Ten years ago school Cadet Corps were few in number, lacking in efficiency, and thoroughly lax in discipline. Routine consisted of some very inert company drills and some very intermittent class-firing, varied by an occasional and very disorderly field-day. Real keenness was confined to those boys who had a chance of going to Bisley as members of the shooting eight. The officers were middle-aged and short-winded. It was not quite "the thing" to belong to the Corps – presumably because *anybody* could belong to it – and in any case it was not decorous to be enthusiastic about it.

But the Officers' Training Corps has changed all that. At last the hand of peace-loving and somnolent Headmasters has been forced by the action of a higher power. Now the smallest public school has its Corps, subsidised by the State and supervised by the War Office. Three years ago, in Windsor Great Park, King George reviewed a perfectly equipped and splendidly organised body of seventeen thousand schoolboys and undergraduates; and these were a mere fraction of the whole. The O.T.C. is undeniably efficient. Its officers hold His Majesty's commission, and have to qualify for their posts by a course of attachment to a regular body. Frequently the C.O. is an old soldier. Discipline and obedience of a kind hitherto unknown in schools have come into existence. That is to say, A has learned to obey an order from B with promptitude and despatch, not because A is in the Fifteen while B is not, but because A is a sergeant and B is a private; or to put the matter more simply still, because it is an Order. Conversely, A gives his orders clearly and confidently because he knows that he has the whole weight of military law behind him, and need not pause to worry about athletic status or caste distinctions.

It may be objected that we are merely substituting a military caste for an athletic caste; but no one who knows anything about boys will support such a view. The new caste will help to modify the despotism of the old: that is all. And undoubtedly the system breeds *initiative*, which is not the strong point of the average schoolboy. In the Army everyone looks automatically for instruction to the soldier of highest rank present, whether he be a brigadier in charge of a field-day or the oldest soldier of three privates engaged in guarding a gap in a hedge. It is these low-grade delegations of authority which force initiative and responsibility upon boys who otherwise would shrink from putting themselves forward, not through lack of ability of character, but through fear of Presumption. And here we encounter another thoroughly British characteristic. A Briton has a great capacity for minding his own business. He dislikes undertaking a responsibility which is not his by right. But persuade him that a task is indubitably and *officially* his, and he will devote his life to it, however unthankful or exacting it may be. In the same way many a schoolboy never takes his rightful place in his House or School simply because he does not happen to possess any of the restricted and accidental qualifications which school law demands of its leaders. Now, aided by the initiative and independence which elementary military training bestows, he is encouraged to come forward and take a share in the life of the school from which his own respect for schoolboy standards of merit has previously debarred him. All he wants is a little confidence in himself and a little training in responsibility. The Officers' Training Corps is doing the same work among public schoolboys today that the Boy Scout movement is doing so magnificently for his brethren in other walks of life.

II

BUT WE need not dip into the future: we are concerned only with the past and its effect upon the present.

What manner of man is he that the English public school system has contributed to the service of the State and the Empire? (With the English public schools we ought fairly to include Scottish public schools conducted on English lines.) How far are the characteristics of the boy discernible in the Man? The answer is:– Through and through.

In the first place, the Man is usually a Conservative. So are all schoolboys. (Who shall forget the turmoil which arose when a new and iconoclastic Housemaster decreed that the comfortable double collar which had hitherto been the exclusive property of the aristocracy might – nay, must – be worn by all the House irrespective of rank?)

Secondly, he is very averse to putting himself forward until he has achieved a certain *locus standi*. A newly-elected Member of Parliament, if he happens to be an old public-school boy, rarely, if ever, addresses the House during his first session. He leaves that to Radical thrusters and Scotsmen on the make. He does this because he remembers the day upon which he was rash enough to rise to his feet and offer a few halting observations on the occasion of his first attendance at a meeting of the Middle School Debating Society. ("Who are you," inquired his friends afterwards, "to get up and jaw? Have you got your House colours?")

Thirdly, he declines upon all occasions, be he scholar, or soldier, or lawyer, to discuss matters of interest relating to his profession; for this is "shop". He remembers the historic "ragging" of two harmless but eccentric members of the Fifth at school, who, dwelling in different Houses, were discovered to be in the habit of posting one of Cicero's letters to one another every evening for purpose of clandestine and unnatural perusal at breakfast the next morning.

If he rises to a position of eminence in life or performs great deeds for the State, he laughs his achievements to scorn, and attributes them to "a rotten fluke", remembering that that was what one of the greatest heroes of his youth, one Slogsby, used to do when he had made a hundred in a school match.

If he is created a Judge or a Magistrate or a District Commissioner he is especially severe upon sneaks and bullies, for he knows what sneaking and bullying can be. For the open law-breaker he has a much kindlier feeling, for he was once one himself. He is intensely loyal to any institution with which he happens to be connected, such as the British Empire or the M.C.C., because loyalty to School and House is one of the fundamental virtues of the public school boy.

Lastly, compulsory games at school have bred in him an almost passionate desire to keep himself physically fit at all times in after life.

He has grave faults. Loving tradition, he dislikes change, and often stands mulishly in the way of necessary progress. Mistrusting precocity, he often snubs genuine and valuable enthusiasm. His anxiety to mind only his own business sometimes leads him into deciding that some urgent matter does not concern him when in point of fact it does. As a schoolboy he was the avowed enemy of all "cads" and his views on what constituted a cad were rather too comprehensive. Riper years do not always correct this fault, and he is considered – too often, rightly – cliquey and stuck-up. Disliking a bounder, he sometimes fails to penetrate the disguise of a man of real ability. Similarly his loyalty to his friends sometimes leads him to believe that there can be no real ability or integrity of character outside his own circle; with the result that in filling up offices he is sometimes guilty of nepotism. The fact that the offence is world-wide does not excuse it in a public school man.

Finally, all public school boys are intensely reserved about their private ambitions and private feelings. So is the public school man. Consequently soulful and communicative persons who do not understand him regard him as stodgy and unsociable.

But he serves his purpose. Like most things British, he is essentially a compromise. He is a type, not an individual; and when the daily, hourly business of a nation is to govern hundreds of other nations, perhaps it is as well to do so through the medium of men who, by merging their own individuality in a common stock, have evolved a standard of Character and Manners which, while never meteoric, seldom brilliant, too often hopelessly dull, is always conscientious, generally efficient, and never, never tyrannical or corrupt. If this be mediocrity, who would soar?